WISCONSIN

IOWA

COL. LINDBERGH'S
BOYHOOD HOME HERE

OLD MAN OF THE DALLES

PRISON

MINNEAPOLIS

WORLD'S
LARGEST MILLING
DISTRICT

ST. PAUL
STATE CAPITOL

LAKE PEPIN

SUGAR LOAF
MOUNTAIN

POTTERY

WORLD FAMOUS MEDICAL CENTER

MEAT PACKING
CENTER

GRANITE QUARRIES

INTERSTATE
PARK

FATHER OF WATERS
MISSISSIPPI RIVER

LAKE
MINNETONKA

MINNEHAHA FALLS

LIMESTONE
QUARRIES

SINCLAIR LEWIS
MAIN STREET

KENSINGTON
RUNESTONE

PHEASANTS

RASPBERRY
COUNTRY

APPLE
COUNTRY

SHETEK STATE PARK
AND LAKE

MINNEOPA FALLS & STATE PARK

LAKE
TRAVERSE

BIG STONE
LAKE

BUTTER TUB OF THE UNITED
STATES

ST STATE IN CORN PRODUCTION

HOGS

1ST STATE IN FLAX PRODUCTION

NE QUARRIES
LD
ATED HERE)

PHEASANTS

HIAWATHA LAND

MINNESOTA SKYLINE

Anthology of Poems About Minnesota

CARMEN NELSON RICHARDS
Editor

Forest, field, and mine enrich thee;
Commerce waits beside thy gate;
Law and learning, art and beauty
Come to crown thee, Northern State.

A. L. MAC GREGOR

THE LUND PRESS, INC.
Minneapolis, Minnesota, U.S.A.
1953

Thirteenth Edition, Revised

First twelve editions published by

THE LEAGUE OF MINNESOTA POETS

FOREWORD

As I read this collection of beautiful poems written mostly by Minnesota people about Minnesota places and incidents, I recalled a visit with a farmer at his home near Northfield. We were standing on the lawn in front of his home. The landscape was transformed by the gorgeous light of the setting sun. He said, "My wife and I traveled this summer. We drove to Washington, thence to Boston, and back home through New York, Michigan, and Wisconsin. We saw many beautiful places." Then, pointing to a tiny valley that was gradually being overcast by the lengthening shadows of the trees on its hillside, he observed, "But nowhere did we see anything to equal that." The little vale was for him a place of beauty made sacred by long familiarity that had grown into a passionate devotion.

Minnesota is a land of beauty, abounding in the romance of life. No wonder that she inspires the songs of poets! And I think this collection of poems about things with which we are familiar will help us to develop a devotion for our home state not unlike the devotion of that humble farmer for his little vale.

W. C. Coffey

President, University of Minnesota.
1941–1945

SONG OF MINNESOTA

Silent forests saw them coming,
Murmured in the red men's ears,
"Look! Behold! Pale strangers venture
Into land you've held for years."
Red men waited, peace pipe ready,
For the strangers to appear;
Feasted them and danced together,
Fought the rapids, hunted deer.

So the trails were marked and opened;
Men brought wives and tilled their lands,
Cut the timber, trapped the beaver,
Dug the ore with eager hands.
Creaking carts from old Red River,
Piled with furs, rolled to St. Paul;
Ore-filled trains chugged from Mesabi
Through the pine trees, straight and tall.

Highways widened over pathways
Trodden by exploring feet;
Skyways beckoned speeding airplanes
Flashing shadows over wheat.
Garnered from the dreams of many,
Built on hopes with courage high,
Grew rich farms, small towns, great cities
Under Minnesota's sky.

EILLEENE SEBASKY KINNEY, *Brainerd*

THE GREAT SEAL OF MINNESOTA

An Indian, mounted on his pony,
Rides full speed toward a setting sun;
Behind him, the white man, bending, plowing,
Visions the glory of work to be done.
His ax, sunk deep in a near-by tree stump,
His heavy rifle, lying low. . . .
Galloping, galloping goes the pony. . . .
"White man here now; Indian must go."

Fainter, fainter, the pony's hoofbeats . . .
Almost vanished, the Indian horde . . .
Freedom! Freedom! The white man's struggle
Still goes on. L'etoile du nord!

GERTRUDE E. ANDERSON, *Litchfield*

HANG OUT THE FLAG
(State Capitol)

Hang out the flag, Son,
This is the day;
Hang out Old Glory, Son,
This is Flag Day.
Oh, look to the sheen of it,
The wind-swept careen of it;
Remember the scene of it —
Boy, it's your flag.

Red for the dead
And the blood that's been shed for it;
White for the right,
Of each fight that's been led for it;
Blue that's as true
As the hue of the sky over it —
Hang out the flag, Son,
Hang out the flag.

It's your flag, Son, all of it,
With a star for each state
In the shade of the fall of it.
Lift up your voice, Son,
Answer the call of it;
This is the day, Son,
Hang out the flag!

STAFFORD KING, *St. Paul*

WHERE THE MOCCASIN
IS QUEEN

(Minnesota State Flower)

A thousand winds have blown through
    sun and rain
To build a loam, to gather leafy mould
For lavish growing. Centuries have lain
In muted melody as thunder rolled
And storms cascaded over every hill
To give the test to trunk of oak and elm,
That fully panoplied grew firm until
They stood as guardsmen in the North Star realm.

Inside the citadel of shade there reigns
An orchid queen in quiet holiday.
Delivered of her purple pomp she deigns
To dress in green as will a forest fay;
She weaves sun-gold into a web for wings
And wins the word of praise from lips of
    kings.

ROSE M. MUCKLEY, St. Paul

QUESTIONS

What do you want to know about Minnesota?
Perhaps of the lakes that lie in the heart of the prairie,
Incredibly blue, or lurk in the sun-drenched hills
Among the ragged ranks of the little oaks,
Of lakes that are lost in the endless hush of woods
Massing around the cradle-shrine of Itasca,
Where the Father-of-Waters sleeps and dreams of birth.
Would you rather hear of the Mississippi himself,
As the tawny waves roll under the thundering bridges
And down below the cities and quiet banks
Where the lingering name, Winona, echoes a legend,
The half-heard whispering ghost of the Indian maiden?
What of the red-wound pits where they scoop the iron,
And the ice-blue air of the lakes, and the sound of barges,
And the shout of trains from Duluth to the echoless plains,
To the very plains of Dakota, or the prairie road
That drops from the hills of lakeland out to the sunset
And loses itself somewhere on the rim of heaven!

ALLEN E. WOODALL,
College of the Pacific, Stockton, Calif.

MEMORIES FROM A FOXHOLE

I miss the beauty of the rainbow trail,
That autumn paints over hill and dale;
I miss the geese honking overhead
And the mallards in the wild rice-bed.

I want the thrill of seeing the deer
With head erect to point his fear,
Or to follow the rabbit's track in the snow
And to hear his thump as he signals, "Go!"

I want the roar as the lake freezes tight
While I stand and wait for the fish to bite.
I have not forgotten in all this strife
How once there was quiet beautiful life. . . .

I would give a lot to be back there
Where God has a hand and seems to care —
But I have memories . . . deep inside,
Where I look, and try to be satisfied.

OLOF M. PEDERSON, *Minneapolis*

ALL HAIL, PIONEERS!

From the low but urgent thunder
Of a stream of wagons wheeling
Like sedate but restless trampings
Of the tireless boots of fate
Came the trader, came the settler
To the virgin woods and prairies
Where the wolf packs and the redskins
Howled their blood lust to the stars. . . .

Came the gambler, came the preacher,
Land shark, merchant, saint, and sinner —
Struggling, crowding, trickling, pouring —
Till the hamlets grew to cities
Vast in wealth and vaster dreaming.

Rouse you, sons of Minnesota,
Carry on the brave traditions!
Keep your heritage unsullied
While the grand old-timers sleep,
While they slumber to the crooning
In the restful sweet disturbance
Of old cottonwoods that whisper
Through the rose-drenched summer nights.

JOHN MORGAN THEW, *Portland, Ore.*

LONGFELLOW'S MINNESOTA

Northward rise the endless forests,
Mighty pines with aspen fringes;
Run the swirling streams and freshets,
Sparkling brooks where trout are leaping,
Limpid pools and falling water.
From Itasca, east, the river . . .
Fountain of the Mississippi;
Westward stretch the sky-rimmed prairies,
Home of partridge, quail, and pheasant.
To the southward are lush meadows,
Cattle grazing in the sunshine,
Golden wheat and tasseled cornfields . . .
Minnesota, where the heart is
Deeply rooted in the northland,
May the red clay of your pipestone
Fashion peace pipes for the nations.

GERTRUDE OLSON, *Winthrop*

Sibley State Park

{13}

PIONEER MOTHERS

You guided the young footsteps of our state,
And taught it how to walk among the great.

From wood and valley, mine and fertile plain
Come tales that prove your work was not in vain.

We know you grieved for loved ones left behind
In other lands, although new friends were kind.

You sang and worked and prayed the months around,
And soon new life took root in fallow ground.

You followed humble paths to higher arts
And shaped the future with courageous hearts.

Today you call across the changing years
To give us strength to fathom new frontiers.

Ten thousand lakes respond in sun-tipped waves
And send a joyful paean to your graves.

EVELYN BYRNES, *Minneapolis*

IN THE SIXTIES

There was never time to play
  For those sturdy pioneers —
Breaking land and building homes,
  Struggling through the early years.

But there were the spelling matches,
  Quilting parties, husking bees . . .
In the school house, built of sod,
  With benches hewn from native trees.

Walking down the lane at dusk,
  Watching hearth fires burning clear,
Homely pleasures, hardships, patience
  Marked the passing of each year.

ROBA BEATRICE WARD, Mapleton

KNUTE NELSON
(1843–1923)

Norseland sired him,
Minnesota claimed him —
Sturdy patriot of an earlier day.
And the land of his adoption
Lifted him high:
Honored governor of Minnesota,
Senator in his nation's service,
Honest man and kindly neighbor,
Close to man and close to God!

MARIE DUGAS, Minneapolis

JOHN LIND

(1854–1930)

Perhaps but few upon our streets today
Can answer, "Who was Lind?" and yet that name
And prefix, Governor, together say
That, while he lived, his world gave him acclaim.

Whoever saw him, stern and dignified,
Might not have thought he was a friend of man;
Yet he had left the narrow groove of pride,
And greatness claimed him for her chosen clan.

With this he had what love remembers long —
The kindness which transmutes dull clay to gold;
No one could doubt that he was brave and strong,
But goodness, too, had deeply rooted hold.

His heart was with the lowly and the weak;
He struck the table with his one-armed might
To emphasize the truth that he would speak
And give to human blindness hope and light.

When Woodrow Wilson sought throughout the land
For one to stay a doctrine's rising wind,
He chose for envoy and for master-hand
The silent, proud, yet common, old John Lind.

ALFRED J. DAVIS, *Minneapolis*

MINNESOTA RAILROADS

Out of the darkness . . .
Its beam's eye flooding the rails
That span the heart of a nation,
Rushes the giant of steel
To reach, in a pattern of timing,
The goal of terminal planning.
Cool and calm at the throttle,
Skilled in the trust of his duties,
The engineer of the railways
Delivers the charges assigned him:
The mail, the fruitage, the people
That link and build on the prairie
A statehood that rises and towers
With natural concord of purpose.
Into the dawn of progress,
The railroads have carried, with valor,
A vital, continuing effort
That breathes of achievement and honor.

FRANCES D. SINGLER, *Los Angeles*

THE MISSISSIPPI

Old Man River rises in Itasca,
Rises in ten thousand lakes, aiming for the sea:
Cass, Winnibigoshish, gem-like Pokegama,
Flowing so the land's rain can at last be free.

Here the brother rivers come — the St. Croix, the Cannon,
The Zumbro, the Root, and the Minnesota's flood;
For Old Man River welcomes to his bosom
The cloudy invisible water that gives wings to mud.

The Illinois comes thundering, the Missouri comes roll-
    ing,
The Ohio, the Arkansas, the dark Yazoo,
Draining half a continent, mountain, prairie, bogland,
Aiming for the great Gulf's endlessness of blue.

Old Man River, born in Minnesota,
Just beneath the Lake of the Woods, the land's northern-
    most reach,
Never forgets the State of his birth — never ceases dream-
    ing
Of bright lakes and Big Woods, oak, maple, beech. . . .

Even out in the Gulf Stream, or the lordly Caribbean,
He leaps up to the sun's kiss, with clouds for his feathery
    wings,
And soars back over bogland . . . prairie . . . mountain . . .
To find again his birthplace, where all life sings.

Old Man River, as the gray skies open,
Rains into his lakes again, far from gulf and sea;
And the glad land's voice whispers the soft message:
"Only in the heart's home can we at last be free."

CLEMENT WOOD, *Delanson, New York*

UNIVERSITY OF MINNESOTA

DULUTH

OPEN-PIT MINE

I SAW DULUTH

I saw, with eyes that had not seen before,
The last faint blush of rose fade from the west;
I let my hand drift idly by the oar
As daylight died, and brought my boat to rest.
Duluth, my city, how you softly rise . . .
Your houses — tier on tier, your hills of green,
Majestic beauty lifting to the skies,
And stretching out beside the lake, serene.
For years I was too blind, too blind to see
The loveliness I held within my hand;
I sought afar to find the ecstasy
That waited here in this my native land.
I felt at last the ageless beauty here
Drive deep into my heart . . . a shining spear!

Dorothy Bladin Hill, Duluth

CITY AT REST

Fog slithers . . . settles . . . hesitates
To lift its vise-like grip
On a night-drenched city
Hunched at the brink of endlessness —
A city quilted in beads of quiet
Punctured by groans from a fog horn's needle.

Ruth Slonim, Duluth

SPRING IN DULUTH

A violent northwester races down
The icy avenues that line the bay;
It whips with fury through the frozen town,
Destroying, mad, unconquered on its way.
I cry aloud that wind and sleet and storm
Have been my bosom cronies much too long!
Where are the moonlit gabbro hills, the warm
And sun-drenched vales of spring, and robin's song?
Then, suddenly, the birds are all in tune,
While laughing zephyrs join their rapturing;
With magic fingertips, a radiant June
Brings hope to life again; my heart can sing.
So does a world of wind and sleet and cold
Become a paradise — of green and gold.

ELVIRA T. JOHNSON, *Duluth*

NORTH WOODS CABIN

A cabin far from the noisy street,
    Apart from weary, toilsome days,
    There we can live in simpler ways,
And feel the grass beneath our feet.

No thought of fear disturbs our rest,
    While stars keep watch throughout the night,
    And shed their clear protecting light
Above our cabin on the crest.

MARY MOORE, *Minneapolis*

LESTER PARK

I love to walk among your friendly pines,
And feel the moss grown thick beneath my feet,
Or view your rivers banked with leafy vines,
Where beavers hew and build a safe retreat.
And here I find wild rose and graceful fern
Or trillium, if I have a mind to seek.
Jack-in-the-pulpit grows beyond the turn
Of lonesome bridle paths above your creek;
And, from a gnarled old tree, a flicker calls
While blue jays chatter in a mountain ash.
In spring, fat trout leap up your swollen falls;
And, failing, back against the rocks they dash.
All this and more I find within your fold;
I love the natural beauties that you hold.

MARGARET D. KENNEDY, *Duluth*

ORE SHIPPERS' SONG

A whistle shrieks, a whistle moans;
The season starts with a million groans.
A ship's hulk looms out on the lake —
Her black smoke trailing, gulls in her wake;
The siren calls, she booms a reply,
The lighthouse blinks its wary eye.

Hear the medley of rugged shores,
Of gleaming multi-colored ores:
The click, click, click of punchers' beats
Like horses' hoofs on cobble streets;
The ship is loaded, the sea gulls wing —
This is the song the ore-men sing.

WINNIFRED ELLIOTT, *Two Harbors*

ST. LOUIS RIVER

Where the black feet of spruces cleave the moss and the
    shadows,
Where the leaf mould crackles under the alder thicket,
I walk in the cool soft light of morning,
And find the beauty of a younger world.

Adventure is abroad, and the sound of singing,
The rhythm of canoe paddles.
I am kinsman to those who journeyed here in another
    time.
I am a priest, a voyageur;
I am one who has gone forth,
Traveling westward to new worlds—
Vast plains, dark forests, high mountains—
From which there may be no returning.
I partake of the spirit of Verendrye, the strong, the
    courageous,
Who gave this river the name of a ruler
Whose guerdon he wore, Louis IX, the Crusader.

Earth is never hurried.
Two centuries ago, they saw
This beauty that I look upon:
The footprints of wild deer on the sand,
The golden flowers repeated in the water,
The air .green with leaf shadows.
They heard the rippled notes of thrushes,
    accompanying their chansons,
Here by the St. Louis River, in the morning of America.

LOUISE LEIGHTON, Baraboo, Wis.

THE EMERALD HILL

(In Memory of Daniel de Gresolon, Sieur du Lhut)

From the days of my youth when excitement ran high
And I answered the stern and provocative cry
Of adventure and zest with a laugh and a will,
I remember the sheen of an emerald hill.

It rose from the waters that danced at its feet
As a generous welcome which rises to greet
A stranger who journeys from far to distill
The wonder and charm of this emerald hill.

It was near there I planted the lilies of France
In the town of Isanti, and knew the warm glance
Of a faithful companion whose presence is still
In the forests surrounding this emerald hill.

There I dreamed of a city whose towers should rise
From the indigo lake to the indigo skies,
And a people whose vision should ever fulfill
The promise and grace of my emerald hill.

MARIE d'AUTREMONT GERRY, *Weslaco, Texas*

Jay Cooke Park

FOG HORNS ON LAKE SUPERIOR

They speak of destinies to me —
Deep-throated voices in the night —
Reporting dangers of the sea.
They speak of destinies to me,
They vibrate with anxiety
To guide boats through the fog aright.
They speak of destinies to me —
Deep-throated voices in the night.

MEDA G. CASLER, *Duluth*

MOONRISE OVER SUPERIOR

Only quiet starlight showed
Cars bordered on the lake-shore road.
For each one, as it parked, would close
Its headlight eyes and seem to doze
Until the moon's thin edge would pull
A tide of homage. To the full,
The watchers saw it grow and make,
Across the dark terrain of lake,
A gold path for a heaven-set tiller.
Like an arc light on a pillar —
Inquisitive, it peered around
Before up-surging with a bound
Into the sky, where it could pour
Benediction on the shore.

EDITH ADDISON THOMAS, *Duluth*

OPEN-PIT MINE

From split earth, scooped,
the iron escaped
and, rusting, ran
from every vein.
Where shovels bite
a deeper pit
in flanks of ground
to chew and grind,
the ore is spilled
and earth despoiled
for bread or hate. . . .
Now, in the light
of smelter fire,
the choice is fear
of men for men:
see how the grin
of leering death
mocks from the hearth!

JESSIE GODDARD BROMAN, *Minneapolis*

STEEL FOR THE WORLD

Monsters! Out of the East they call for steel —
For ore and coal to eat, to smelt, to make the steel molten.
Monsters of the East that turn to the ranges of Minnesota—
To the Vermilion, the Cuyuna, the Mesabi.
There the pits, like craters of the moon,
Open to the summons and give their precious ore
To trains and steamers — slaves of the East.
Down the grade come the cars, pulled by blackened
    slaves,
Sweating, rumbling, toiling, rolling to Duluth!
Malleys — huge and cumbersome — coming to Duluth!
There the inland port of ore
Barters with the East: ore for coal — coal for ore,
Dealing in the hugeness of Vermilion, of Cuyuna, of the
    Mesabi . . .
Down the shafts, in the holds, ore like Solomon's gold,
Rumbling, groaning, crying, traveling to the East —
By lake freighter, across lordly Superior,
Past the locks of Sault Ste. Marie, to Lake Erie, to Pitts-
    burg,
To the East.
Ore! Brown ore, dirty cold ore,
Shoved, shorn, and shackled,
To make steel for America —
    Steel for the world!

                              WILLIAM A. SOMMERS, *Duluth*

MISSABE ORE DOCKS AT NIGHT

Docks like giant centipedes
Boldly stalk into the Lake.
The inky water at their feet
Is satin-smooth and seems to break
In patterns like brocade . . . moire . . .
As lights reflect down on the Bay.

Rows of lights that line each edge
Are scintillating diamond chains
Looped from standards down the length
Of dock, to guide the heavy trains
That, heavy-laden, carry ore
To pour in boats there by the shore.

Docks in daytime are immense
Structures of steel . . . their girders strong.
At dusk, with ropes of lights along
Their rim, reflected in the Bay,
They wade on stilts in black moire.

I marvel how a thing all ugliness by day . . .
At night becomes brocade and magic . . . and moire.

LUELLA BENDER CARR, Proctor

LAKE SUPERIOR FISHERMAN

His face is grim, his mouth is grim,
And his eyes are grim as the graying sea;
He casts his nets where the herring swim,
As he takes his chance with destiny.
The fruitful lake is his only bride —
A woman of many moods is she,
And many are those she has cast aside
As she beats her bosom savagely.

Like a sea gull perched on his rocky ledge,
Snug in his one-room hut is he;
He mends his nets at the water's edge,
With his pipe and his cat for company.
Then he dreams and plans for a future day,
When his silver catch has brought him gold,
Of a trip to his homeland far away,
Of the crystal fjords and the mountains cold.

How can he guess that the jealous lake
Will hold him fast with her siren song,
That, from his dream, he will awake
To the sound of her storming, wild and long?
The fruitful lake is his only bride —
A woman of many moods is she,
And many are those she has cast aside
As she beats her bosom savagely.

HELEN JENSWOLD DAHLE, *Duluth*

NORTH SHORE OF LAKE SUPERIOR

The road winds in and out along the shore:
Now over sharp-split rocks that seem to rise
Unbidden from the ground, while giant firs
Patrol the ragged miles of wind-swept beach,
Where strong-winged gulls, in lofty circles, soar
Around the isles which rest serene and calm
As shadows on a peaceful mountain pool.
The road glides smoothly on: a sudden glow
Where goldenrod salutes us as we pass;
We thrill with joy when birches, pale and white,
Gleam suddenly among the darker trees —
The maidens of the forest, coy and shy,
Who hide beneath their veils of quivering leaves.
We top a hill and suddenly we glimpse
A flash of water, clear and blue, amid
The pines. A strange elixir, mingled scent
And light, fills all the lambent air, and still
The road winds in and out along the shore
And beauty hallows the enchanted scene.

L. Eleanor Voswinkel, *Kansas City, Mo.*

Gooseberry Falls

*Splitrock
Lighthouse*

BEACON OF TRUST

As vessels daily leave Duluth,
    A signal flares before,
That clearly marks safe paths for cargoes
    Bound toward a distant shore —
A beacon guide to mariners
    Like Athena's fire of yore.

Just as this light of ancient days,
    Which kept the seaways free,
Undaunted by the waves that lashed
    To windward and to lee,
So towers Splitrock Lighthouse high
    Above our northern sea.

                MARJORIE HERRMANN COX, *St. Paul*

LAKE SAGANAGA

Beside this lake when autumn shades
Are echoed in the placid bay
And stars come out as twilight fades,
I think the earth has stopped to pray.

Cathedral calm of holy trees,
Where wood-folk bow their heads in prayer,
Shall give us faith as well as these,
Inspiring us to worship there.

When stars like altar candles shine
And send a beatific ray
Through dim arcades of singing pine,
I think the earth has stopped to pray.

                LESLIE L. CODE, *Minneapolis*

LADY SLIPPERS

Lady slipper, have you danced
  On some Indian maiden's feet,
In the ghostly moonlight pranced
  To the tom-tom's measured beat?

In the fragrant summer nights,
  Did you climb the moonbeam — high,
Keeping time to Northern Lights,
  As they swished across the sky?

Lady slipper, did you care
  When the spirit, watching, found
You were too inclined to dare,
  And pinned you to the solid ground?

GRACE A. SCHAEFER, Minneapolis

THE CAMPER

Across the lake a campfire gleams,
Some camper sits and smokes and dreams . . .
  Give him of your strength, my forest,
  Share your patience, make him whole;
  Deep lake, with your cooling waters,
  Soothe his spirit, cleanse his soul;
  Cloudless sky, restore his vision
  Shaded by a city's dust;
  You, my wild friends, teach him honor
  By the fullness of your trust.
Across the lake a campfire gleams;
Good camping, friend, and pleasant dreams.

JEANNE SHOWERS KNOOP, Side Lake

ARROWHEAD AISLES

Come, let us walk among the somber pines —
They seem to beckon toward their peaceful aisles,
All carpeted with rugs of green and brown.
Our footfalls make no sound nor leave a trace,
And fragrant shade invites to quiet thought.
Here is a glade where fern and columbine
Nod to their pictures in the placid pond,
Which mirrors smiling skies and fleecy clouds;
And here a doe, watchful of eye, steps out
To lead her dappled babies to the rill
Which glides into the pond with murmuring song.
The sun is sinking. Hear the vesper songs
Of birds that seek their nests. Come, let us go —
The cabin hearth-fire beams a welcome home.

LILLIAN REIQUAM SANDBERG,
Dearborn, Michigan

A HUNTER'S DREAM

Line on the rod and gun on the shoulder,
In dreams we tramp as we grow older;
Closely we follow the trail of the deer,
As we climb the hill, over cones and boulder.
Back are the days we were younger and leaner —
Eyes to the morning and ears to the night —
Breath comes fast and senses keener. . . .
Who can be calling us? Why the delight?
Old urges quicken to harden our will:
Voices are calling us — calling us still!

GEORGE EDWARD HOAG, *Minneapolis*

BORDER BALLAD

The sun is slanting his August rays;
Over its boulders, the river runs slack.
Days to come are wilderness days,
We are free to follow the waterways
With paddle and compass and bulging pack.

Como, Lucerne, and Windermere
Are too well known and too long tamed
For any man who has portaged here
And felt the pines pass dark and near
Through lakes in thousands, carelessly named.

Wind blows down from the far-off pole,
Waters swell to meet each stroke,
And the eager day runs on to its goal
Where blankets lie on a frosty knoll
In a forest blue with bacon smoke.

BETTY BRIDGMAN, Minneapolis

AWAKENING

The fern
Shoves tiny fists
Through loam — much as a tot,
Waving rebellious clenched fingers,
Awakes.

MABEL ENDRESEN MILLER, Winona

RECOLLECTIONS OF A NORTH-WOODS HOMESTEAD

Out of the past, mixed memories I keep —
    The cold, clear brilliance of a winter night,
The wolves' wild chorus rousing us from sleep,
    The frost-rimmed windowpanes, the flickering light
Cast by the fire of birch and tamarack
    (Our first line of defense, if laid with skill)
When Arctic night beset the rough-hewn shack,
    Inexorable, and eager for the kill!

       *   *   *   *   *   *

June, in the Big Fork valley, brings a lush
    Exotic growth. The almost-tropic sun
Leaves, to a darkened earth, a sensuous flush
    That stays until the new day is begun.

       *   *   *   *   *   *

Each was concerned with how the other fared;
    It seemed the patient brutes, who pulled the plow,
Were one with us . . . each loss or gain was shared —
    Our tenets would no preference allow.
Admitting but the peace that follows toil,
    Our struggle with the complicated scheme,
By which men wrest a home from virgin soil,
    Now seems part stern reality — part dream . . .
Real as the scars we bear, dreamlike as fear,
    When that which threatened is no longer near!

Dana Kneeland Akers, *Superior, Wis.*

LAKE VERMILION

HIGH FALLS ON PIGEON RIVER

ST. CROIX RIVER

TAYLORS FALLS

Climb higher and higher in the Dalles of the St. Croix
Until you look over the jutting cliffs
Of echoing beauty, the great eternal mounting
For a village linked and timed with history.

The years have passed since eighteen fifty-one:
Taylor has gone but the falls roll on—
The crowded water roaring, swirling,
And pulsing with memories of the past.
The giant pines no longer groan, "Log in a jam!"
While the sawmill gnashes its teeth
Above the steamboat landing.
No longer the blasting charges
Drown the voices of loggers and waters.
But lonely and majestic moves the breeze
Above the pot-holes and the Devil's Chair
Of a village albumed in history.
The Dalles House, which heard
The voice of Douglas, Lincoln's rival,
The church, the library, the power dam—
All mark the passing of time.

Daringly I step, wishing to ascend the Pulpit Rock
And place a flower there in reverence
To still-arched beauty
That has watched a village grow!

PEARL NEARPASS, Minneapolis

Interstate Park

THE MILLSTONES OF THE GODS

The gods, in the throes of experiment,
For countless eons toiled to see
The valley's tortured surface rent
Into a scenic rarity.

From icy tongues three glaciers dripped
Their shallow streams across the beds
Of lava. Slowly rivers ripped
Basaltic rock to terraced treads.

By swirling eddies, rock-bestrewn,
In swiftly flowing water, round
And round were rolled the millstones, hewn
From granite ridges, glacier-ground.

Into crystalline rocks were drilled
Unnumbered pot-holes, deep and sleek.
The Dalles at Taylors Falls fulfilled
The quest the gods forever seek.

ANNA WILHELMINA WHITCOMB,
Minneapolis

MY HOME TOWN

(Taylors Falls)

Proud may they be that call this grandeur home:
    These rocky cliffs, gigantic boulders, dells,
    And mystic caves beside the swirling waters,
    The wooded banks, and dark bottomless wells . . .
Here nature flourishes in wild abandon:
    In new-green Junes, or gaudy autumn hues,
    Or in the still white beauty of December,
    In sunset reds, or silver morning dews . . .
This is my hometown, here are faithful friends,
    And houses rich in hospitality.
    There is a glory here and loving welcome,
    That warms me with its glowing memory.

ANNE AYDT CARON, *St. Paul*

OUR POETS

The bird and the poet,
That sing from the pine
To the plain, re-echo
The songs of the heart;
But the river and the rose
Sing the songs of silence
That are too deep
Or too beautiful
To be told in words.

    ETHEL MARY DAVIS, *St. Paul*

Interstate Park

W. H. C. FOLSOM
(1817–1901)

A man of vision who dared to dream,
He left New England for the Northwest;
The years of his life held only one theme:
"Faith in my country, God does the rest."

He cared not for fame, nor chose to be rich;
The State Park shared as his homestead grew.
He saved for youth the lands for which
The schools are still drawing their revenue.

He helped to design Minnesota's Seal,
To civil justice he lent his weight;
For centuries will our people feel
His personal impress on our state
DOROTHY E. GRAFF, *Taylors Falls*

FROM A BUS WINDOW

St. Croix State Park

The clouds are playing checkers
    Upon the fields I pass —
First, one moves . . . then, the other . . .
    With shadows on the grass.

A square of darkened clover,
    One took before I came;
But I move on too swiftly
    To see who wins the game.
IRMA M. PATCH, *Minneapolis*

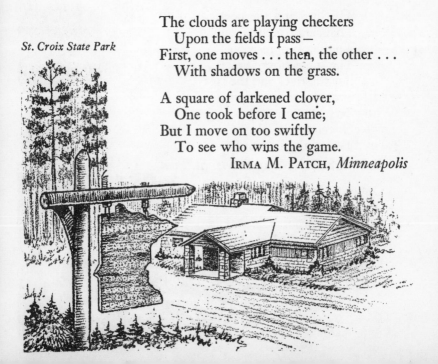

THE HINCKLEY FIRE
(1894)

A demon swept across our land of pines
To ruin, with fiery breath, the trees and vines.
He clutched, with blazing fingers, old and young;
He lapped the waters with his flaming tongue.
In hopeless grief, strong men and women wept
When smoke had smothered babies, as they slept.

The sons of pioneers had grubbed and toiled
To clear the land for homes, that fate despoiled.
A brush could never paint the spectral view;
A pen could never tell how terror grew —
Domestic animals, song birds, and game
Were found where they had perished in the flame.

The engineer who raced his train with death,
The fireman who worked with gasping breath,
With other helpers — eager, brave, and strong,
Forgot themselves to aid the frightened throng.
They reached the lake to end their frantic dash;
The train that carried them then burned to ash.

The Hinckley Monument, gift of our state,
Arose in dignity to commemorate
The names of victims. Many hearts yet hold
A deeper grief that lips have never told.
Though wounds were keen and vivid scars remain,
The years have mellowed memories of pain.

NORA BYRNES HEGI, *Minneapolis*

{43}

DELANO ON SATURDAY NIGHT

The old bridge groans beneath the constant weight
  Of town-bound traffic as the cheerful noise
Of creaking axles, auto horns, and motors
  Is blended with the shouts of girls and boys.

Carloads of country folk and laden trucks
  Line up along the narrow village street;
The stores fill up with happy eager shoppers;
  The sidewalks feel the print of many feet.

Men, bent with toil, feel younger in the glare
  Of lights, exchanging jokes and arguments;
And women brighten as they meet and talk
  Of recent births, and brides, and home events.

Tall boys and girls in the first flush of love
  Fill the "coke" bars and laugh at everything —
Their eyes revealing dreams within their hearts,
  Their voices thrilling to the songs they sing.

Saturday night in town: a whole week's labor
  Repaid by sharing joy and grief with friends.
Cars piled with packages, they turn to home,
  And so another gay adventure ends.

MARGARET HORSCH STEVENS, Montrose

AUTUMN AT ANOKA

Break not the magic of my dreams,
  Speak no soft word, give no heart's token;
Leave me these rolling hills, these fields and streams
  Where God's great silence is unbroken
Save by a startled note of thrush,
  Or cricket chirp or whir of wings;
Leave me these tranquil trees that hush
  Their whispering when my heart sings
In muted caroling to burnished rose
  Unveiled in this still woodland shrine
Where I have worshiped beauty. Never close
  These glorious autumn dreams of mine!

FLORENCE KREEGER HUNTING, St. Paul

SUNFLOWER SEED

Here life is sleeping in a silver case,
Transmuted metal . . . out of yellow gold,
To wait until the bugles of the spring
Awaken life along the country road.
Then shall arise the legions of the sun,
Following time . . . and beating golden drums.

EDWARD VAN ANTWERP, St. Paul

NOT BY BREAD ALONE

With bread, not stone, we answer every cry
Of distant nations: "Help us lest we die!"
  A thousand smoke-filled furnaces, ablaze,
  Form warp and woof for all production's maze;
  The woodsman's strokes fell mighty forest trees
  To fashion ships to range the seven seas;
  And to complete this trinity of toil
  Is nature's largess of our fruitful soil.

But more than this: here man's inertia breaks
Amid the glitter of ten thousand lakes,
  Where Isaac Walton dreams again his dream,
  Gloating over the yield of lake and stream;
  And peaceful woodlands and a gentle breeze
  Content man's soul and bring his senses ease.
  Here in this mighty state, we long have known
  This truth: "Man shall not live by bread alone."

WEBSTER E. SMITH, *San Diego, Calif.*

REVERIE IN THE MINNESOTA VALLEY

Hidden in the branches of an old oak tree,
A brown thrasher sang to his love and to me.
I lay with the grass, long and soft, for my bed
As I dreamed in the blue of the sky overhead.
Could there be a heaven beyond that bright sky
Where souls still live when their bodies die?
I think that my spirit would steal back to be
In a bed of green grass with a bird and a tree.

MURIEL CADWELL SOLETHER, *Minneapolis*

TO THE MINNESOTA RIVER

You knew the red man, his tepees, arrows,
And merciless prowess in battle.
You bore his canoe on your bosom
When the oar hardly broke the silence
While the brave and his plighted maiden
Were whispering dreams to each other.
You saw the coming of the white man,
The building of cabins, the turning
Of the long dark furrows that omened
The worth and the wealth of your valley.
Then you heard the drums of the Dakotas,
Their war cry, and the screams of women
Who fled from the torch and the rifle;
You knew Other Day and Medicine Bottle,
The friend and the foe of the settlers;
And Old Bets, the sad fate of her lover,
And her loyalty, long and lonely.
You must remember LeSueur and Sibley,
The Traverse des Sioux Treaty with Ramsey,
And the dance and the feast that followed.

There is lore where you have been winding —
Tales of suffering, sorrow, and progress;
And you, as you flow by heavy harvests
And cities that teem with toil and culture,
Must wonder what magic has molded
The dreams and the deeds of a people.

EDWARD COLLINS DOWNING, St. Paul

SUMMER DAY AT MINNETONKA

O life, that days like these might last!
Time's dial crowds the hours too fast
To drink life's nectar to the brim
Or chant in full the evening hymn.

Frail silver cobwebs in the morn
Swayed gently as the day was born;
Tall lindens with their clusters, sweet
With honey, fanned the noontide heat.

As twilight falls, when cares grow less,
Across the lake, with soft caress,
The moon looks down amid the vines
Lighting a thousand wayside shrines.

Dear God, that days like these must pass!
Too soon the sand runs through the glass.

ESTHER FRIEDLANDER, *Minneapolis*

STORM AT MINNETONKA

A furious wind races across the lake;
The waves leap and lick at high banks,
A murderous green and black.
Do not dare to step into nature's war,
Or be deafened by her battle cry
And blinded by a beautiful streak of light,
Bursting, flashing like a crater in the sky —
Sometimes like a many-fingered hand,
Turning and twisting cruelly . . . .
Stop, wind!
In that angry embittered strength
There is tyrannical rhythm
Of the ghostly incessant beating of waves —
Waves of storm beating
Against the rocks of the proud point,
Against the pale sand of the smooth shore.
No Indian maid is laughing here,
But an ancient foe, terrible in derision!

LILA CLAIR GROSS, *Minneapolis*

PASQUE FLOWER

Dainty little pasque flower,
First messenger of spring,
You are very clever
For such a tiny thing;
For though you wear a party gown —
A gown of silken dainty mauve,
A cozy fur coat keeps you warm
Against the chilly wind and storm.

MIRIAM AUGUSTA COMPTON, *Minneapolis*

BY EDINA MILL POND

Down the slope at the water's edge
Stands a tall blue flag in the waving sedge.
Over the pond the black terns call,
And a song sparrow trills from the old stone wall.

Above the water the swallows skim;
The bittern wades in the marshy rim;
Bulrushes nod in the quiet stream,
While high overhead the hen hawks scream.

The sunfish watches his nest in pride;
A shiner flashes his silvery side;
And the pool, with the face of an impudent lass,
Gets it slapped by the tail of a big black bass.

The sun is warm with a friendly smile;
A cricket strikes up on his musical file.
We can hear the bees on the clover heads,
And breathe the fragrance the wild rose sheds.

The echoes still come from across the pond,
Still the whippoorwills sing in the wood beyond;
The waters escape with their old-time roar . . .
But the mill they once turned is heard no more.

EDITH M. SCHUSSLER,
OTTO F. SCHUSSLER,
Minneapolis

HENRY HASTINGS SIBLEY
(1811–1891)

"Wah-ze-o-man-zee," Walker in the Pines,
So you were named, friend of the Indian.
The long trails of forest, hill, and prairie
Had beckoned here your young and restless spirit;
And you found work to do, far beyond
The bartering of furs and hunting of game.
Lonely journeys filled your days, far from home
And family, as you brought law into the wilderness.
You found your brother, the Indian,
Needing a clear voice in the halls of Congress;
You were not afraid to defend the weakest
Of your neighbors.

You built well, O pioneer,
A house of sturdy oak and stone
In the valley of Mendota,
Where majestic waters meet.
But stronger, more enduring was your house
Of high endeavor. You built — with deeds
Of justice, friendliness, and courage —
A firm foundation for our growing state.
Hunter, trader, soldier, statesman — you served
Your country well!

GENEVIEVE R. BREEN, *Minneapolis*

WHEN LARKS HAVE SUNG

"What do you like the best about a farm?"
I asked you, who know intimately all
The ways of it, and you said, "Well, the small
Things coming up in order, in the warm
And moistened spring — the miracle of growing."
And I agreed, and knew you did not mean
Specifically *grains*. For I have seen
You watch a swallow, with the sunlight glowing
Upon its breast, come back to feed its young
As if you heard "La Golondrina" played;
And I have known you, when a pheasant laid
Her eggs, to guard them; and, when larks have sung
Across a meadow, all the world has dropped
Away for you until the chiming stopped.

ELAINE V. EMANS, *Hutchinson*

TREES

I marvel how the elms can grow
For years and not complain
Of autumn's sleet and winter's snow
Or April's pouring rain!

Their beauty lures us in the May
Beside the road and hill
Where robins build their nests and sing
When dawn breaks cool and still.

WILLIAM ALLEN, *Faribault*

STILLWATER

In a quiet friendly valley
Lies a quaint historic city,
Nestling on the St. Croix River
Like a gem set in the hillsides.
Long ago, the old men tell me,
Indians roamed this peaceful valley,
Sioux fought Chippewa and slew him,
Where this peaceful city rises.
Now the ancient oaks and maples
Glorify its streets and byways;
And, in nearby woods and valleys,
Flowers bloom in wild abandon
In a symphony of color.
Here the skies seem always bluer
In the afterglow of sunset;
Here the evening stars shine brighter
And, reflected on the water,
Gleam like diamonds spread on velvet.
Here the earth seems nearer heaven,
And the cares of life rest lighter
In the friendly quietude.
How I long to stay forever
Here within this quaint old city,
Nestling on the St. Croix River,
In a quiet friendly valley.

HOPE STEWART HANNAH, *Stillwater*

POWER

Moveless he stands against the iron railing,
With all the world about him in commotion.
The mighty water races on beneath him
To storm the falls. From the unnumbered chimneys
Flutters the smoke in long wind-shredded pennons.
The switching engines, blowing clouds of steam,
Tear back and forth, while over its granite arches
Thunders the night express, steady as fate,
With pomp of banners and proud illumination.
On every hand is power visible,
And yonder where the mills and powerhouses
Are lighting up their tier on tier of windows,
Intenser it moves in spinning shaft and wheel,
Or lurks disguised in sleek and humming turbines.
Yet in that quiet figure by the railing,
Frail as a wisp between the sky and water,
Labors the sovereign force of all the planet.
Master of all the powers of earth and air,
He well may gaze upon his harnessed river
And stand unmoved amidst the hurly-burly.

JOSEPH WARREN BEACH,
University of Minnesota

MINNEHAHA FALLS

MINNEAPOLIS

MINNEAPOLIS

When up and down the "Shining River"
Trapper and trader, priest and Indian
Sent their canoes — then I was born.
The voyageurs called me "Village of Falling Waters."

In those far distant days,
I called my children to the river's side;
And now, in countless numbers, they have come
Who toil and build and here abide.

My fairy towers uplift their lofty heads
While stars shine through the marbles, tessellate;
And splendid spires in silence point to God,
His name to celebrate.

My emerald draperies trail the river paths
And border lakes strung as a rosary,
Translucent pools, and classic falls,
Where dwells a wealth of poesy.
Beauty is my great heritage, and I claim
That boundless beauty for my deathless fame.

No longer "Village of Falling Waters,"
I now am known as "Lady of the Lakes";
Ceaseless their murmur and their gentle fret —
Proudly I wear you, O my waters,
My sapphire coronet!

GRACE UPDEGRAFF BERGEN, *Minneapolis*

MINNEAPOLIS MINIATURE

These are the things I love the most:
Clean water, long cool nights,
The smell of smoke from burning leaves,
The city's twinkling lights,

Wet pavements, rain upon my face,
The night wind in my hair,
The smile that glows in friendly eyes,
A baby's solemn stare,

A dancer's slender gracefulness,
Low voices — sweet with song,
Thick shining hair, all dogs, all trees,
And arms — if they be strong.

If there be things more beautiful
Than these, let me not know,
For fear I might be surfeited
With life — and go.

LEITH SHACKEL, *Minneapolis*

THE SYMPHONY

From out the ages comes the need
To reach beyond our microcosmic lives,
To feel the overtones of universe
That lie within our beings —
Strange chemistries are mixed in sound.
Known, yet unknown life there is
Within the harmonies and rhythms
Of the larger sphere;
And we reach out
Through music's subtle guide,
To gain some touch with greater things that are.
Rare beauty — ugliness are found.
Sudden joy, quick gloom —
The lightnings and the wild free winds
Of fancy carry on.
The tangibles with intangibles
Are woven for us on a loom of sound,
And those who listen
Find new meaning in their lives.

A. RUSSELL BARTON, *Violist,*
Minneapolis Symphony Orchestra

AUTUMN TUMBLEWEEDS

Rolling
Tumbleweeds, like
Old men, hasten to the
Wind's music — the singing tempo
Of fall.

ORPHA GULLICKSON, *Fertile*

IN THE BASILICA

Dim and vast, the twilight aisles —
Dim and vast, the vaulted roof —
Amethystine shadows, deep,
Caress each pillar and high arch,
And kiss the wounded feet of Christ.
One deathless gleam of holy light
Leaps up to touch the Crucifix
Above the sacred resting place
Of Him who daily dies for us.

    O Blessed Lord, at Thy dear wounded feet,
    I lay the burning fever and the ache
    Of all this sin-stained, dusty day,
    And, kneeling, crave Thy Father-touch of love!

Then soft upon my jaded soul,
Thy peace that passeth worldly ken,
Like healing dews on wearied flowers,
Gently falls upon my heart.
A lonely worshipper I came;
I go, deep solace in my soul.

Dim and vast, the vaulted roof —
Dim and vast, the twilight aisles —
Amethystine shadows, deep,
Clustering thick in every arch,
Jewelled now with Holy Light!

Anna Augusta von Helmholtz-Phelan,
University of Minnesota

MEMORIAL DAY SERVICE
(West High School, Minneapolis)

I Pledge allegiance to the flag . . .
Said an old man ninety-five . . . a thousand young . . .
Grayling teachers . . . a bombardier come home . . . mothers
With wounded eyes . . . the speaker . . . a nisei . . .spatterings
Of World War Ones . . . said it for Bill and Bob and Jim,
Memories of twenty years and more.

Of the United States . . . and the Republic . . .
In the dim meeting place, people still rise in May —
Hands pressed to hearts — voices, tremulous and low.
Would they in dust could see the lilaced loveliness
Diffusing Minnesota spring, hear taps bugle-echoed,
Wipe tears from burning lids, smile at wreaths
To girdle crosses named for Bill and Bob and Jim.
Our love pours out . . . and now some lonely little boys,
Star-lustered only yestereve, join them in honor.

One Nation . . . with liberty and justice for all.
They might, even as you, have built strong towers
Against the sun; plowed earth made sweet by summer wind;
Gone home to God in native soil geraniumed with love,
But not more mourned. Their mothers hold the token rose
For Bill and Bob and Jim . . . and for the youngest. . . .
Compassionate God, heal these wounds, too,
Of both the living and the dead.

WANDA ORTON, *Minneapolis*

THE MINNEAPOLIS PUBLIC LIBRARY

Here magic windows behind brownstone walls
  Open upon a fairy land of dreams,
  A land of quiet meadows, cooling streams,
Deep forest paths, and silvery waterfalls;
Of long-forgotten cities, whose old halls
  Have high-arched ceilings built of blackened beams.
  Here Rembrandt's mystic inner sunlight gleams
On armored men and women in quaint shawls,
And here are quays where boats with colored sails
  Discharge exotic cargoes from far shores:
  Rich ivories and gems, baskets of ores,
Old wines in earthen jars, and silken bales . . .
  Through rainbow-hued enchanted panes he looks
  Who is at home in this great House of Books.

EMMA BELLE YOURDON, *Minneapolis*

FOSHAY TOWER

The Foshay Tower, standing strong and silent,
Keeps watch above my city;
And, like a slender finger,
Touching the clouds in beauty,
It points the way to heaven.
From its thousand windows, warm light glows
And melts the darkness of the black night sky.
It stands serene and still —
Of the city, yet above it,
Sending its beacon rays across the earth
And heavenward, reaching ever to God.

NANCY COOSE, *Minneapolis*

MARIA SANFORD
(1836–1920)

How do you know
That any one is great?
When you are young, I mean,
And none has told you
That a quiet voice
And ways devoid of affectation
Are true signs.
We often watched her
Studying in her library
Like the professor that she was,
Or working in her garden:
Pruning her lilac trees,
Training her clematis.
We saw her trundle her wheelbarrow load
Of books from her house to the campus;
And, when she smiled at all the children,
We felt that she was kind.
We should have known that she was great
From the glory in her eyes.

ALICE O'CONNELL SHERMAN, *Minneapolis*

NOCTURNE

Decrepit arc
Of streetlamp streaming
In a dingy park.

Among fallen leaves
Curling for warmth,
Rising by starts unwarmed, the wind grieves.

On benches late
The transient shapes of men
Wait — wait.

Moonlight carves
The laggard forms.
Shadow wraps their dinginess in scarves.

RAY SMITH, *Minneapolis*

AUTUMN QUIET

A galaxy of sunset stars·
Drapes every oak tree bough,
The maples like red candles burn
Against the hilltop's brow.

A frosty wreath of pinewood smoke
Curls softly on the hill —
I listen for the cricket's chirp,
But all is hushed and still.

BLANCHE HUNTZICKER, *Mankato*

IN LORING PARK

Weekdays in a quiet park
With new-white swans
Upon a green lagoon, people talk
To a one-legged soldier feeding crusts to birds;
Children run, yelling with outstretched arms —
Clothes pressed taut by the wind —
And singing of life and freedom like uncaged birds.
Upon the hard-worn benches sit the old ones,
Soaking brittle bones in pools of youthful sun,
Disregarding coarse-carved mottoes on their
   painted thrones,
And dreaming only of the days that were.

At the end of the day,
The somber shapes hurry, homeward bound.
To cage the young, to comfort the old,
Fretfully to mull the problems on their hands
And worry —
It takes silent courage and a certain heroism . . .
It needs weekdays in quiet parks, with swans
Upon the green lagoons — and someone throwing
   crusts to the birds.

ELEANOR ROTHENBERGER, *Minneapolis*

{ 65 }

MILLS ON THE MISSISSIPPI

They stand like monuments of time,
Built from the teeming, yielding soil,
Towering on the river front —
The fruit of pioneering toil.
And, from this busy inland port,
Their products journey round the earth,
And with them go a state's proud name,
That formed the cradle of their birth.

LIANDRA PENN, *Minneapolis*

TO WILLIAM WINDOM
(1827–1891)

Since you have crossed the chasm into another sphere
And yet can sense the fever with which we strive,
Assist us to a course of duty without fear
That to nobler ends in life we may arrive.

And though the years succeed each other, one by one,
The example of your life stays fresh and clear.
Oh, true — your mortal work is over, the sands are run;
Still those things for which you lived are always near.

ROGER L. WINDOM, *Orlando, Florida*

TO MY FATHER, P. M. DAHL

(Pioneer Civil Engineer and Surveyor)

My father was a pioneer
  From Norway's ancient land;
He had the wisdom of a seer,
  And skill of eye and hand.
Surveying endless forest tracts,
  He laid out boundaries,
Recording measurements and facts
  In courthouse registries.

In Minneapolis today
  His dreams are realized;
Its noble streets and parks display
  The beauty that he prized.
The city seems to speak his name
  To all his sons and daughters;
And could man wish for greater fame
  In this great City-of-Waters?

BORGHILD DAHL, *New York City*

THE GHOST OF ST. ANTHONY FALLS

This is the chant of Anpetusapa,
Wailing the dirge of the Indian maiden;
This is the one who goes with her sorrow,
Goes with her children, her heart heavy-laden.

Here in the hours of the early morning,
Sad-eyed, and seeking a watery ending,
Swiftly she flees from her mate in the wigwam,
Fleeing the new wife with stoic pretending.

No more to follow him through the dark forest,
No more to wait while the campfire is dying —
In her canoe beneath the fierce rapids,
Bright in her buckskins and beads she is lying.

This is the story of Anpetusapa,
This is her ghost where the great mills are grinding,
This is the legend of the Dakotas,
Haunting forever the river's slow winding.

ADA CLARKE CARMICHIEL, Minneapolis

NAMING ST. ANTHONY FALLS

In sunset clouds above the falls,
I see, reflected there,
The daring feet of questing men
On trails the red men share.

They do not march in rank and file,
With martial music playing,
But step to a new-born river's song
And pine trees' rhythmic swaying.

The first who comes is Radisson,
To lands few feet have trod;
Then, after him, comes Hennepin
To teach the word of God.

He hears the meaning in the music
Of the waters as they fall,
So names them for St. Anthony,
On whom the trusting call.

KATHERINE B. McCORMACK, *Minneapolis*

INDIAN MAIDEN AT LAKE HARRIET

Tell me, black-eyed Indian maiden,
   Did you breathe this scented air?
Did you pluck white-petaled blossoms,
   Tuck them in your braided hair?

Did your lover steal up softly,
   Close behind you on this path,
Guessing fingers on your eyelids . . .
   But you knew him by his laugh?

Did you walk around the lake, then,
   Hand in hand, as we are now;
Sit, perhaps, as close together
   Here on this worn willow bough?

Stay a moment, timid maiden . . .
   Ah, I probed her past too well;
I have come too close to guessing
   Things she did not want to tell.

ADA GREINER MARKS, *Minneapolis*

AS THE WIND

Willows, like young maidens,
   Unruly as the wind,
Weep and sigh and follow
   After the brook.

CORP. LAURENCE E. ESTES,
     Gowen Field, Idaho

SNOW ON LAKE HARRIET

The snow comes down in slow and sodden flakes
To brush with white the trunk of every tree,
Thick-laid on twigs to veil the rounding lakes,
Where yesterday my walk had taken me.
So much is hidden from my morning view:
Slim bushes purified with mantled snow,
Late reddened ripe by autumn as he flew,
Like lovers who leave wounds and swiftly go.
How white the snow! How distant is my spring —
A chord of music that my memory plays —
Lost while fast-falling snows to branches cling,
Like days that pile on years and years on days!
　Silent the snow comes, sudden is its fall,
　Suddenly years make silence of us all.

MARGARET REDDING LAPPIN, *Minneapolis*

LAKE OF THE ISLES

Little shining racing waves,
Shimmering in the summer sun,
Eager seeking avid mouths,
Lapping up the sand in fun,

Are you always greedy, restless —
Do you never, never sleep?
Are you trying ways to travel
Where the bed is cool and deep?

Keep your troubled day of doing,
Little waves of gentian blue;
You will come to deep-sea ending —
Time will have its way with you.

ETHLYN WIGHTMAN WHITTIER,
Minneapolis

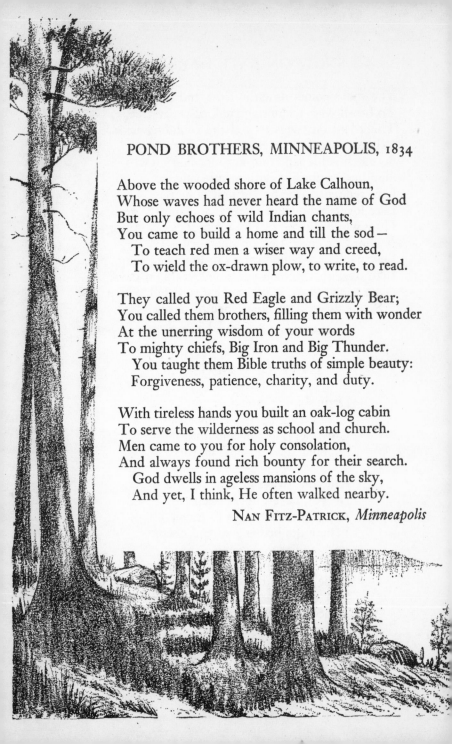

POND BROTHERS, MINNEAPOLIS, 1834

Above the wooded shore of Lake Calhoun,
Whose waves had never heard the name of God
But only echoes of wild Indian chants,
You came to build a home and till the sod —
   To teach red men a wiser way and creed,
   To wield the ox-drawn plow, to write, to read.

They called you Red Eagle and Grizzly Bear;
You called them brothers, filling them with wonder
At the unerring wisdom of your words
To mighty chiefs, Big Iron and Big Thunder.
   You taught them Bible truths of simple beauty:
   Forgiveness, patience, charity, and duty.

With tireless hands you built an oak-log cabin
To serve the wilderness as school and church.
Men came to you for holy consolation,
And always found rich bounty for their search.
   God dwells in ageless mansions of the sky,
   And yet, I think, He often walked nearby.

NAN FITZ-PATRICK, *Minneapolis*

FORT SNELLING

A round stone tower with long slit eyes
Watches them come . . . watches them go . . .
And looks, inscrutable and wise,
At gallant marchers, row on row.

W. D. Frye, Cambridge

THE STATE CAPITOL

ST. PAUL

TREAD OF TIME

(The Mississippi Speaks to St. Paul)

I am the river
And I roll on,
On to New Orleans and to St. Louis.
Great city, I have watched you
Since steamers have plowed through my waters,
Laden with trinkets,
Crowded with people
Who were frightened at the sight of the Indian.
I have watched you grow up, little city,
Grow up nervously,
Away from the little log chapel —
Always reaching out —
Away from wharves,
To the railroad, to the airplane
Till you lost my timeless rhythm.
How I long to rise and roll through you,
If only to feel your pulse — I know your heart;
But I have no time — no time, great city;
I must roll on,
On to St. Louis and to New Orleans.

MARY JANE RYAN, *St. Paul*

VETAL GUERIN, VOYAGEUR

Beyond his mud-chinked cabin's door
And windows and its puncheoned floor,
Beyond the frontier campfire dreams . . .
Indians, forests, swamps, lakes, streams . . .
Beyond Fort Snelling . . . ox carts . . . all
That picturesquery, St. Paul,
He saw a vision. His little town
Had vanished like an autumn's brown,
Scarlet, and gold! In Guerin's eyes
A city loomed with enterprise!
Timber wolves' howling, hungry beasts' prowling
  Had gone like clouds in widening skies.

And Vetal Guerin, voyageur,
Forgot the trapper and the fur.
His gliding boat had heard a song
Of rippled sunlight . . . shadows — long,
Yet rainbow-winged, and starred. He saw
A courthouse rise in stone, with law
And order paramount, and he
Glimpsed a cathedral, yet to be —
Thanks to his aid. It was his part
To give his city half his heart . . .
Timber wolves' howling, hungry beasts' prowling
  Had gone, and progress nurtured art.

Robert Cary, *St. Paul*

JOHN IRELAND, 1838–1918
(First Archbishop of Minnesota)

Indians stalked the dusty roads
    When Ireland came across the seas
To this far western wilderness
    To build a church and colonies.
He fought the ignorance of men,
    He struggled with their doubts and fears,
He fought intemperance and sin —
    Blazing a trail for future years.
He founded schools for boys and girls,
    His talks and writings brought him fame,
He welcomed settlers from the East,
    And all the country praised his name.

And when his eighty years approached their end,
The whole state claimed him as a sage and friend.

                 LAURENE TIBBETTS, *Minneapolis*

SUMMER

Summer
Has quiet nights
When star-curtains hang low,
Draping the heat of the day in
Cool dusk.

            OLGA SELKE, *St. Paul*

ISAAC LA BISSONIERE, AT EIGHTY, RECALLS OCTOBER OF 1841

We saw the new young priest come paddling back
In his white birch canoe, as we took guns
Along the Mississippi bluffs or sloughs,
And knew his hands were blistered from the task
Of taking his good folding altar round
To even St. Croix cabins up the stream.
We really ought to build a house of God
Since we had Lucian Galtier come from France,
But winter leaps upon the very heels
Of northern autumn—that must wait for spring.
So thought the elders; we who were eighteen
Turned from the red deer and south-pointing ducks
To raise the tamarack rafters, lay the floor,
And sing the oak walls up, all sound and sweet,
On land and with the logs the settlers gave.
We beat the snows in that squeezed space of time,
Eight eager lads. Swiftly the chapel rose—
St. Paul, we called it from a church in Rome.
Though no one thought this wilderness would see
A city born upon the selfsame spot,
Yet I have seen it grow in very truth.

EMMA M. LARSON, *St. Paul*

THE CATHEDRAL OF ST. PAUL

What majesty arrests the roving eye,
Ascending where the city's barter ends!
What deep and peaceful splendor shares the sky
Above a winding thoroughfare that sends
The humbler avenues to homely peace.
Below, the great industrial fires roar
Commands that whirring gears shall never cease;
Yet smoke from throbbing stacks floats out to pour
Its homage at God's footstool, the broad crest
That holds the font which gave the city its name . . .
Here let the hungry saint and sinner rest
For nourishment, and let youth's ardent flame
Burn as a vigil torch . . . Here is no night!
Angels bend low before the Eternal Light.

HELEN LETHERT MEIER, *St. Paul*

TO FRANK BILLINGS KELLOGG
(1856–1937)

He ventured half the world and all of heaven
To make one blazing, bright experiment.
The wretched dough which never felt his leaven,
This he ignored. Meanwhile, equivalent
To his exacting thirst for fellowship,
Kindred minds awoke eager to taste
The chalice of the ages, lest it slip
From nerveless fingers to the sands of waste.
And when, at last, he sought the eye of God,
Expecting little less than blighting doom,
Lo, it was dimmed with weeping, and the rod
Of judgment shook and burst in fragrant bloom;
And half the world and all the heaven he lost
Before his feet a victor's tribute tossed!

GEORGE L. WAITE, *Marietta*

FULFILLMENT

A hand, a head, a heart indeed are ours,
A great triumvirate of perfect powers.
Each by itself will never reach a goal,
It takes all three to make a perfect whole;
For earthly deeds are only nobly wrought
When love and care we add to work and thought.

ORRIN J. RICHARDS, JR., *Grand Marais*

A SPIRE AT HAMLINE

I sought for something sweet to chase
Reality away from me:
I read of love, of Helen's face,
A pastoral, of Kilmer's tree.

I searched for humor, tried to sing;
I built a castle in the air.
I gazed at Rembrandt, tried to bring
Into mind the beauty there.

Then suddenly my fears all died —
I saw a spire against the sky,
Raised for a cross, a mortal's guide,
To life most holy, life most high.

I faced reality with peace;
I knew that love would live again
And war and hate would some day cease —
This spire, a symbol, not in vain!

DORIS ANDERSON RICHARDS, *Grand Marais*

MINNESOTA BATTLE FLAGS FROM GETTYSBURG

See how these flags by grievous gaping wounds
Retell the battle and the glory!
Though dust falls thick on distant graves and grasses —
Dust unto dust, yet here is all their story.

Their fabric stained with blood, and worn and old,
Mute emblems torn by shot and shell,
They saw that fierce and sacrificial field
On which, to save the Union, brave men fell.

And on that field where war's grim flowers bloomed,
Still running where the bright flags led,
A soldier of the line, in lasting bronze,
Commemorates for us our gallant dead.

Let memory forever closely cherish
These flags our North Star state holds dear,
For those from Gettysburg which led the men
Of Colville, in Minnesota's First, are here.

Let them grow old but never be forgotten,
Beneath the Capitol's vast dome;
At Gettysburg their work long since was finished,
And now they rest — their labors done — at home.

HATTIE S. BORDEWICH, Minneapolis

APOSTLE OF THE HELPLESS
(Dr. Arthur Jay Gillette, 1864–1921)

There was no school in all the world
   For these young wounded things,
No sheltering place within the scope
   Of their clipped wings.

    "We are not responsible," the public said,
      "For casualties of nature or disease,
        No way to care for them except by one and one,
        No wider scheming can there be for these."

Alone you found their plight
Not hopeless, bleak, without redress . . .
You pioneered with service, pen, and word
Until there rose on Phalen's shore
A monument to hope.
Within four walls,
Encompassing a home and school
And doctor's care, were born bright gleams
Of future usefulness and health.
Today a trusting host of eager mended youth
Survive in glad fulfillment of your dreams.

              HELEN IRENE GARVEY, *St. Paul*

FLYING THE BEAM

White sea gulls are wheeling above ice-blue marshes,
Betrayed by warm winds which enticed them to roam;
But soon they will follow the fast closing river,
And, southward, will faithfully be guided home.

Dear lad, far away, you fly into the morning —
Young hands steering true, keen blue eyes alight —
But when dusk rolls up fog, or storm signals give warn-
   ing,
On the beam of my love, fly home through the night.

FRANCES GREENLEAF JENSEN, *Hastings*

FLOODTIME IN MINNESOTA

The mighty Mississippi flows bank-full
Where Hastings' ancient spiral bridge resists
High winds and storms — the ever-threatening pull
Of mad and tumbling waters. Spray-filled mists
Steam over Minnehaha Falls, whose roar
Again is heard above Twin City noise
As its cascading fabled waters pour
On stones that might have been a giant's toys.
The spring released the frozen floods of winter
To fashion lakes where last year's meadows lay;
Their sun-warm depths contain no icy splinter
To warn the wading heron's hapless prey.
But when the floods recede, the sun's great power,
As in the days of old, wakes leaf and flower.

MARY FARRIES, *Hamel*

STRANGE BEAUTY
(In Governor Ramsey's Home)

So this is the beauty authentic —
  The beauty art critics demand!
White roses! We say they are common?
  Oh, no, for these roses will stand
The chisel, the heat of the fireplace
  As drawing-room guests understand.
And these wonders of art are environed
  In a dwelling historic and grand.

Marble bushes, with roses outstanding
  Beyond *bas-relief*, fully blown,
Reveal a gift stranger than fiction —
  A hidden art vein little known
Till this master of pioneer statecraft
  Was twice given the governor's throne!
Now the iron-fenced lawn and the mansion
  The state should be happy to own.

W. C. A. WALLAR, *Minneapolis*

MY OAK TREE

No pictures hang upon my walls;
But, etched upon my window pane,
Tall against the winter sky,
An oak tree stands, head tossing high,
As if to chide the blustering wind.

IDA F. WYATT, *Minneapolis*

PALACE OF ICY SPLENDOR

What words can do you justice,
What phrase can quite express
The glamour of your colors,
    Your frozen loveliness!

You stand in frosted splendor,
You awe each passer-by
With pastel shades of sunset
    Etched against the sky.

A fairyland of crystal,
You stand in bold relief;
Unlike the ancient castles,
    Your beauty is too brief!

HARRIET KNIGHT SALVAGE, *St. Paul*

A FRINGE OF SNOW

With early morn there came a heavy snow;
And, as I walked, the flakes clung to my lashes;
But, lo, when I shook off the laden fringe,
There fell to earth a dust of silver ashes.

GLENNYS BALSKE, *Minneapolis*

WINTER'S LAST EMBRACE
(Como Park)

The last snow patch around the edge grows dark,
Relinquishing its whiteness to the sun,
To the soft winds that come to woo the stark,
The bleak indifferent trees, until undone —
Winter's last embrace!
               A wild bird flings
Three fluted notes of fervor through the air,
And soon the brightness trembles with soft wings,
And wild spring noises echo everywhere.

Intensity prevails . . . the heavens burn
With deeper blue; a quiet wonder fills
The twilit air, while, soundlessly, an urn
Spills amber stars above the shadow hills,
The silent lake, the trees of feathery haze.

The lamps drop gleaming pillars in the lake
And slowly drain my eager, breathless gaze
Of comprehension . . . Then my senses wake,
Breaking the spell, and so, remembering,
My heart and mind turn once again to spring.

VICTORIA JANDA, *Minneapolis*

EDITH GUSTAVSON

SUNSET MEMORIAL PARK

Beside the pulsing highway
Where I pass each day,
There rest the dead.
And, as I hurry by,
Intent on my own little world,
I hear, above the noisy din of hurtling speed,
The singing silence of the dead.
I slack my speed;
I pause a moment
As the dizzy round of daily life
Goes reeling past. Where was I hurrying?
The dead once hurried, too, but now they rest.
One should be glad to sleep
Where beauty blossoms in the scented dawn,
And tears of yesterday are lost
In purple shades of everlastingness.

DOROTHY MILBRATH HALVOR, *Shakopee*

MY COTTONWOODS

Only when
The wind whips
Through my cottonwood
Trees, and flips
Their leaves do I remember
Their silver shining
Underlining.

IRENE MORTENSON BURNSIDE,
Denver, Colo.

THE STEAMER *CAPITOL*

Great swan of our river,
Floating symbol of summer,
I have seen you from the edge of dawn,
Throughout the purple evening,
In the murmuring dark,
Heaving with pleasure.
I have seen your gilded plumage
Reflect the moon and sun,
Or meet the buffets of storm,
As you trailed pearls and flowers
In the racing foam.
Amid strains of laughter and dance,
As your huge body pulses,
Romance is born —
Aged hearts are lightened.
Great veteran bird,
Loved Mississippi swan,
Float on!

ALICE BARR, *Minneapolis*

CLIFFS ALONG THE MISSISSIPPI

These rocky ranges built against the sky
Of opalescent clouds, that hide the sun,
Are set in deep foundations. Reaching high
In cliffs of yellow limestone, everyone
Strikes far into the earth. An eagle's nest
Is hid among the crags. Rough, chilly feet
Of hills thin-veiled on naked back and breast
Are bathed in rivers kind with summer heat.
This little part of our Great Builder's task
Is told in reckoning the seven days
That were Creation. We, in wonder, ask
How many eons, what computed ways
Accomplished earth and sky and boundless sea.
The answer rings from star-filled space, "Eternity."

EMMA KINNEY WHALEY,
Palo Alto, Calif.

MUSHROOM CAVES

White sandstone bluffs,
That tower haughtily,
Enfold in their deep heart
A gentle alchemy.
Here mushrooms crowd
The twilight solitude,
Transformed by mystic rites
To precious tangy food.

MARJORIE KNOWLES, *St. Paul*

ALONG THE MISSISSIPPI

WINTER

A PALACE OF FROST

Out of the shadows of nowhere,
In the stillness of the night,
The fingers of dusky artists,
With flaming strands of white,
Needle to each bush and tree
A cover of crystalline dew
And hang on fences silently
Many a pale festoon,
Making, of the catkined
And grass-entangled slough,
A glittering palace underneath
A limpid winter moon.

RUTH SMITH EWY, *St. Paul*

MISSISSIPPI MOOD

April's ice is a fairy boat,
Put in for moonlight fuel;
Dawn on the river sets afloat
The craft, with steersman's duel.
Deep, the current's mighty flow
Insists, too, on contention;
Mischief-making sun cries, "No!
Heave ho, my mates, attention!"
Torn asunder, each wee raft,
Ablaze with jewels — rainbow-blending,
Struggles now both fore and aft . . .
And comes at last to a watery ending.

LEILA M. STICKLES, *Red Wing*

FRONTENAC INN

Frontenac Inn is an old, old woman,
Squatting on the shore — Pepin lapping at her feet,
Looking down her nose at the upstart moderns,
With a sulky ear for the Sankey music's beat.

Drowsing in the shelter of the high green hilltop,
Whence the Indian maiden won her bloody fame,
The old inn dreams and is more than half persuaded
She lived through the eons till the white man came.

She saw black skirts pushing through the mossy forests,
Bearing a cross to win a savage horde,
Scorning the terrors of the virgin woodland
To win copper saints for the glory of the Lord.

She muses, half smiling, on those Orlean dandies,
Beating up the current, a jest to mask their will.
What god had gilded the prize worth their enduring —
A tiny fenced enclosure where their bones lie still!

NAN M. CLARK, *Minneapolis*

READS LANDING

Reads Landing calls to mind again
The pontoon bridge where frontier men
Came to meet the boat, to walk
And trade and talk.

For though these men have gone to rest —
Like ice, upon Lake Pepin's breast,
That sinks beneath warm April rains —
The bridge remains.

A. PHIL LONDROCHE, *St. Paul*

LAKE PEPIN

Within its loving cup of green,
  A priceless bit of jade,
    Leaf-embossed,
The Never-Never turquoise sheen
  Is shot with lapis shade.
And memories of budding May,
  All happy things that were,
    Dreams long lost,
Are borne upon each jewelled spray,
  As they had blossomed there.

When has not beauty called the soul,
  Like chapel bells, to prayer?
    They truly kneel
Who look within the great jade bowl,
  Though it be unaware.
A blessed peace comes over them,
  A peace they never knew;
    The Christ is real.
Each wavelet wears a diadem
    Of pearls and diamond dew.

NELL MABEY, *Frontenac*

John A. Latsch State Park

WINONA

Have you seen Winona, where the waters spread
Round the ancient gravel fill of the river bed,
Where the Mississippi pauses in its flow
Past the spurs of riven cliff down to Trempeleau?
This was once an island — south of Castle Rock,
Where the sheer and frowning hills break and interlock —
Sleeping in the sunshine when the land was new,
Island home of Wapesha, chieftain of the Sioux.

North of Minneowah was the trysting place,
Famed in song and legend-lore of a vanished race.
Here beneath the headlands, sure of fish and game,
Gathered all the wandering band when the winter came.
Here the smoke arising from the tepee poles
Mingled with the river mist at the fishing holes.
Here the fair Wenonah, keeping rendezvous,
Won from death immortal fame . . .legend of the Sioux.
Now a modern city fills the island space;
People drawn from many lands throng its market place.
Save romantic story, that its name retains,
Nothing but a memory of the past remains.
But, in every springtime, violets awake
Under cliffs of Sugarloaf and along the lake,
And the spell of beauty, ageless, will endure,
Cradled in the circling hills, changeless and secure.

MARK L. ROWELL, *St. Paul*

Garvin Heights

WILD GEESE OVER WINONA

Last night wild geese were over Winona,
Wheeling and crying.

Against luminous clouds,
The light flaring up from the town
Transformed them to gold:

Gleaming golden necks
And fleeting golden breasts
And beating golden wings—
Bright moving gold against a dull gold sky.

Beautiful, bewildered,
Held in by the light
And not daring the dark,
Till dawn they circled the city,
Crying.

     W. E. BOOTS,
     Winona State Teachers College

WENONAH

Above the castled heights that skirt Lake Pepin
Looms Maiden Rock, precipitous and gray;
From that high craggy dome, thus runs the legend,
An Indian maid, love-harassed, leaped to death.
Wenonah, fairest of Keoxa's daughters,
Untutored but by wind and sun and rain,
Learned the word to which her soul responded,
And gave her life to prove her knowledge true.
Her burning heart held kinship with great Sappho,
In tune, as hers, with love and poignant grief.
Though centuries of time divided them,
Her life, not less than that sweet Grecian maid's,
Was poured in full libation at love's feet.

SISTER M. PASCAL, *Rochester*

HOMEWARD IN HOKAH

If heaven be no more than a village street,
And going there be just a walk along its way
In the low sunlight of late afternoon,
    Homeward at close of day,
  Past little houses under roof-trees' glimmering smile,
With blue smoke climbing from each chimney tip,
Good supper smells and quiet white doors, waiting,
And, on the lawns, gay children and glad dogs in
    Swift companionship —
If heaven be only this, I say,
It could not be a better close of day.

EDITH THOMPSON, *Houston*

Beaver Creek Valley State Park

{98}

NIAGARA CAVE

(Near Harmony)

By sturdy wooden stairways we descend
Into the earth's cool vaults . . . with curious eyes
Explore strange corridors that curve and bend
Through towering walls. We marvel at their size.

Here we behold a thing of ages past;
Amazing masonry lies all about.
The eerie scene unfolds, sublime and vast,
While we are lost in thought, the world shut out.

The hand of man has lighted up these walls
Where time's unhurried fingers left their mark.
We hear the roar of water as it falls —
A river disappearing in the dark.

For centuries Lost River must have swirled
Through layers of solid rock by devious ways
To sculpture this fantastic hidden world
Whose artistry calls forth the poet's praise.

A liberty bell, a high cathedral dome,
And fossil forms intrigue us as we pass;
In echoing halls where restless waters foam,
Stalactites hang like spears of milky glass . . .

All this beneath a pasture . . . not a trace
Of rocky cliff or ledge to lend a clue,
Yet far below in this bewildering place
Mere man with time may hold a rendezvous.

LUCILE CHANDLER, *Minneapolis*

WINTER NIGHT AT AUSTIN

The moonlight reveals
A quilting of snow
That covers the trees
And the valley below;
Not a single star
Is hidden from sight,
And the white-rimmed brook
Is contented tonight.

On muted wings
The breezes woo
The rising smoke
As it reaches the blue;
In a playful mood
The shadows fall. . . .
But the world is at rest —
Unaware of it all.

J. A. RANUM, *Austin*

MINNESOTA MOON

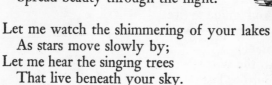

Let me dream, O Minnesota moon,
  Beneath your mellow light;
Let me walk where northern pines
  Spread beauty through the night.

Let me watch the shimmering of your lakes
  As stars move slowly by;
Let me hear the singing trees
  That live beneath your sky.

Let me watch the Mississippi flow,
  Flow onward to the sea;
Watch dainty lady slippers bloom,
  That touch the heart of me.

O Minnesota moon, you always leave
  My soul a hallowed scene,
As your rays of light reveal
  What joys of heaven mean.

CLARA A. CLAUSEN, *Kenyon*

GRAIN TREASURY

The wheat is falling — golden rain
That fills the chutes of storage towers
To swell the river of the grain,
Sun-warm from Minnesota's fields.
The city's treasury is filled
With shining coin the rich land yields.

LILIAN OSBORN, *St. Paul*

HIGHWAY BUTTONS

Buttons . . .
Down
The spine
Of the highway's
Busy line —
They fasten a curve
To every hill,
And kindle to fire
At a motor's will.
Stars . . .
In the west —
Buttons lost
From Hermes' vest,
They mark the highways of the sky
For the moon's round wheel
To travel by.
Markers
For men,
Coming, going,
Home again!

MARTIN HALVERSON, *Austin*

WIND IN THE CORN

Grey streets
grope like tendrils
through the endless twilight
of brick and mortar valleys . . .

I remember the moist, yolky
smell of plow-turned earth.

Strange white grubs
feed steel-fleshed gods,
that rasp and snarl their
song of triumph . . .

I remember men who walked in the sun.

Plaster skies,
forty watt suns,
love by proxy with celluloid puppets . . .

I remember the shadowed
stillness of a moon-drunk country night.

A million plodding footsteps,
a million dream-dead eyes,
a million haunted faces,
a solitary heart . . .

I remember wind in the corn.

DICK NELSON, Winona

THE GIANT PEN
(To O. E. Rolvaag, 1876–1931)

His New World saga, "Giants in the Earth,"
Portrayed so vividly our pioneers
That I, with them, suffered the throes of birth
And death. I, too, endured and conquered years
Of blizzard, hail, and drouth. And more, I thrilled
To find there tales my father told—the sound
Of myriad geese, the cranes and ducks he killed,
The prairie fires, the hopper-scaly ground—
Even the winter known as "the big snow."
Here was a deathless epic of those days
That tried my stalwart forebears long ago.
And it was Norway's son who rendered praise
To his new land, to immigrants, to men
Like mine—long rooted here. Oh, giant Pen!

ELOISE WADE HACKETT, *St. Paul*

HENRY BENJAMIN WHIPPLE, 1822–1901
(Apostle to the Indians)

"There was a *man!*" The old chief's sunken eyes
Lit inwardly as recollection shone
On Whipple's name—the red man's champion—
Staunch warrior in a cause he made his own.
Though gently bred, he braved the wilderness,
Bishop of pioneers—of gracious touch,
Friend of the lowly, great among the great.
Fame was his acolyte and only prized as such.

FLORENCE GIBBS KEENAN, *Minneapolis*

WINTER ROAD TO ELGIN

Telephone poles are the mark
Of country roads when new snow hides
The last sleigh-runners' parallel track;
Against the white they stand like guides
To point the way to town and back.

Country roads are lonely roads
When winter's soul lies pale and still
And buildings of the scattered farms
Seem huddled close against the chill
Of frosty penetrating charms.

It seems a sacrilege to mar
That untouched surface; but my team
Goes wading through without regard
To sentiment, hauling the cream
To market though the way is hard.

DONALD M. HEIN, *Elgin*

IN MEMORY
of Drs. Will and Charlie Mayo

Close ranks — press ever onward, men in white —
The road is long, the battle still not won;
Two men who led you are beyond your sight,
Trusting to you the deeds they left undone.
Conceived in chaos, a vision came to life
Beneath their hands of heaven-guided skill;
Before the hardest task, the deepest strife,
They lifted valiant spirit, dauntless will.
Their shining guidance is before you yet,
Pointing the way that follows God's true plan —
You and a saddened world will not forget
The two whose hearts held first the need of man.
  In humble prayer, for these two lives, give thanks. . . .
  Then, shoulder to shoulder, men in white — close ranks!

MARJORIE W. BRACHLOW, *Minneapolis*

FROM MY WINDOW
(Rochester)

A morning sun shines through my windowpane
To show a Sabbath day in vivid gown;
Beneath a cloudless sky, in queenly reign,
October flashes yellow, red, and brown.
Then mellow chimes, from Mayo clinic dome,
Give golden sound to pattern beauty's weave,
As if the angels, from their distant home,
Lent voices to the notes the bells achieve.

How graciously this city of great healing
Accepts the tribute that I offer, kneeling.

N. MARGARET MYERS LAWRENCE,
Nashwauk

ORIGIN OF THE MAYO CLINIC
(Tornado — 1883)

Out of the violence — malevolent, sweeping,
Out of disaster and anguish and weeping
Came help for the sick, ease for the dying . . .
    And science and knowledge.

One with skill to heal stood like a giant;
Found for his helping the gentle, reliant,
The nuns of St. Francis, who questioned and comforted —
    Seeking to aid.

Strange that the elements' furious raging
Should hold at its center the whole world's assuaging!
Should raise — from the wrack, the tempest, the turmoil —
    A blessing for all!

            HELENBELLE KLIER, *St. Paul*

ROOT RIVER

Along the banks of bold Root river,
Their roots washed bare by tides and sand,
Are towering oaks with leaves a-quiver
Like fingers on a grandfather's hand.

Gnarled and twisted, they bend to catch
The river, flowing warily by;
But stiffened clutches are no match —
The stream slips on with a taunting cry.

        HAZEL KING TJEPKES, *Stewartville*

Oronoco Wayside

CITY OF HEALING

Greater than her ten thousand lakes,
Farther renowned than groves of gale-swept pines,
Or trails where red men stalked the living meat —
These do not bound her glory!
All countries have their sacred pools,
Pan-haunted groves, and ancient streams
To give men passing pleasure and restore ebullient life
To summer's rest, to autumn's angling, and to winter's chase.
But when life's power wears out in use
With toil and love, with sacrifice and play,
Then failing hearts turn trustful eyes
And lift their voices in final prayer to Rochester:
Here is the shrine of men who willed their Godlike service
To recreate the broken lives that come
For restoration to this City of Healing.

JOSE BOSLEY, *Mitchellville, Iowa*

BEAUTY BUILDS

We build with patient art
Each town, machine, or plan.
When beauty fills the heart,
It blesses every man.

EVELYN ELSTER, *Minneapolis*

Whitewater State Park

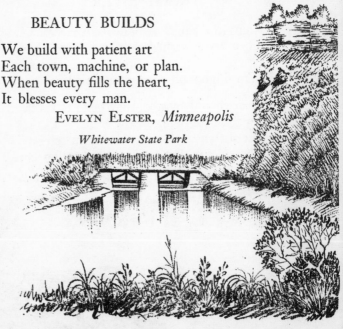

ROCHESTER

PIPESTONE QUARRY

PIPESTONE NATIONAL MONUMENT

(Birthplace of the Peace Pipe)

The chieftains and the tribesmen of this land
Still love a shrine where red men come to pray.
A small deep glen is cut through rocks that stand
On either side — tall sentinels of gray;
And, through this gorge, a little streamlet sings,
Then makes a leap from off the pipestone ledge —
A sparkling, dancing waterfall, with wings
That fly to keep the ancient red men's pledge.

This pledge is kept by smoking pipes of peace
Carved from the quarries, just as years ago;
And tomahawks, and bows and arrows cease
To terrify our land today. We know,
On cloudy nights, the campfire's flames reveal
The faces of departed braves, who sit
In circles, with their calumets, which seal
The pledge — a mystic brotherhood, close-knit.

These sacred tribal councils of the braves,
That Chippewas, Dakotas, Sioux all share,
Give approbation for the pledge that saves
The peace for noble red men everywhere.

FLORENCE ENGLISH HADDEN, Minneapolis

WIND OF THE MATAWAN PRAIRIE

O summer wind, blow gently
Across our prairie land;
Touch all the flowers lightly
That bend beneath your hand:

Blue iris in the meadows,
Wild phlox along the way . . .
In the early morning,
The scent of prairie hay.

Wind, now cease your moaning —
Give me a moment's rest!
Turn your wild weird sighing
Into a merry jest.

For, though we tame the prairie,
The wind we cannot tame,
And flowers blown too often
Can never be the same:

Blue iris in the meadows,
Wild phlox along the way . . .
And, in the early morning,
The scent of prairie hay.

EMMA D. BABCOCK, *Faribault*

LAKE OZATONKA

This land was once a lake whose waters gleamed
  With rice, where flocks of mallards fed at dawn;
Here Indian braves in birch canoes sought out
  The trout's cool haunt, the lair of deer and fawn.
This lake reflected many bloody moons
  As war cries sounded in the long ago
Across the pale sands washed by angry waves,
  When arrows flew against a hated foe.

But now rich farm lands stretch on every side,
  And lanes of ditches cross its placid face.
Here corn lifts up its silken tasseled head,
  And man's skilled work is noted every place.
Today old buried arrowheads of flint,
  Turned by the plow, alone recall the story,
Once echoed in the hunter's fearless call,
  Of wild free days and red men's ancient glory.

MADELINE WEAVER, *Easton*

Camp Release Wayside

{113}

TREATY OF TRAVERSE DES SIOUX

(July 23, 1851)

Minneopa State Park

Here on a famous battle ground,
Where Sac and Fox had met the Sioux,
Where Sissetons and Wahpetons
Conquered their enemies, and slew
The hostile tribes for miles around,
Five thousand warriors met the whites,
In eighteen fifty-one, and sold
Two dozen million acres, with rights
Of hunting and of furs, for gold.
Feathered like eagles were the chiefs,
And solemn were Ramsey and Luke Lea
As legal seals, in duplicate,
Translated this to history.
Only a name is the "Crossing" now,
Only a relic, the treaty, too . . .
Only the wind in the grass is sighing —
Or is it a homeless Indian, crying!

MARY SALINDA FOSTER, *Mankato*

Minneopa Falls

{114}

AN OLD, OLD TREE
(St. Clair)

An old, old tree in an old, old town —
   A treasured relic of things long gone —
   A monument whose count of years
      The winds of chance cannot regain.

It lifts its arms to high blue skies,
   It sings with winds, it laughs with showers,
   And nesting birds the summers long
      Have gently mellowed its refrain.

Here men and women have lived and loved,
   While children have laughed the hours away;
   And village folk have sought its shelter
      In time of sunshine, in time of rain.

An old, old tree that has weathered the years,
   It stands a monument of might,
      Nor storm, nor power of earthly thing
         Has ever challenged its domain.

                              EDITH FOSTER CHASE, *Mankato*

Alexander Ramsey State Park

PIONEERS OF SOUTHERN MINNESOTA
(Eagle Lake)

My father was a pioneer
With head erect and courage flaming;
His brawny arms and mighty ax
Cleared the land with furious taming.

One hundred men made up his crew
To fell the trees and pile them high,
To melt in smoke as the engines ran
Through towns that grew as they passed by.

My mother baked a barrel a day
Of flour in golden crusted loaves —
What miracles of food there came
From ovens of those old wood stoves!

Thomas Reeves and Sarah, his wife,
Were giant folk in a noble band;
They carved a place in the solemn wood,
Made fruitful fields in a virgin land . . .

To them I make acknowledgment:
Before their shrine my head is bent.

LEAH MAY STEPHENS, *St. Paul*

Mound Springs

BLUE MOUNDS NEAR LUVERNE

Proudly rising above the plain,
Immune to sun and wind and rain,
These scattered rocks and towering wall,
Like silent witnesses, recall
The history and ancient lore
Of ages vanished long before.
Here are legends carved in stone
That, once, forgotten men had known.

The rocks would tell you, if they could,
What happened where they long have stood:
How frightful monsters roamed this place;
When first they saw the human race;
How once the red men with great cunning
Started herds of bison running
Over their cliffs to death below,
Where heaps of bleaching bones would show.

But all the secrets they have known
Are safely kept with tongues of stone.

CARMEN SUURMEYER, *Luverne*

SPRING ON THE PRAIRIE

(Walnut Grove)

Look, the awakening comes without a sound;
The ice-ribbed wheat field sighs and breaks its bands;
A woman walks the furrows, thrusts her hands
Into the healing sweetness of the ground. . . .
Here, in the silence of this spring, I found
Peace for the winter heart, a faith that stands
Firm as the promise of these prairie lands,
That stretch away to sunset — emerald-crowned . . .

There is assurance in a head bent low
Over the fragrant path of loose rich loam:
A lasting pact between God and a man,
Within the seeds he covers row by row;
A sign that, though pain mark his narrow span,
Earth still is kind, is still his dearest home.

VALERIE SIMMONDS, *Minneapolis*

SUNSET ON A REDWOOD FARM

Softly the evening sunset
Scattered its golden beams
Over the fields and forests,
Over the lakes and streams.
Even on humble hilltops
Wonderful scenes unfurled . . .
Looking like thrones of angels
In a celestial world.

DIDRICK J. ORFIELD, *Minneapolis*

*Birch Coulee
State Park*

THE BLUE EARTH MEETS THE MINNESOTA

Flowing, newborn, through the silence
That knew not its birth nor its coming,
It cradled in soil so tinted
The sky seemed imbedded within it.
Rippling with freedom of motion,
While rounding a bend in the woodland,
It met with waters more rampant,
A river more boastful of spirit,
Who, seeing the youngling approaching
And sensing that nature had willed it,
Purled to his bosom the streamlet
And eddied with joy through the outlet.

*   *   *

Here where waters bring coolness,
A playground of green has been builded,
Where flowers and laughter of children
Re-echo the spirit that crowns it;
And, though old settlers, convening,
Recount how red men had named them,
Only the cosmos of silence
Remembers the wedding of rivers.

LILLIAN ATCHERSON, *Minneapolis*

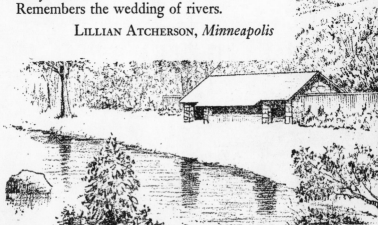

Camden State Park

BIG STONE LAKE

Along the western line of Minnesota,
   There Big Stone Lake in shining splendor lies;
Across the silver waves of liquid beauty,
   The bluffs of South Dakota etch the skies.

As high winds blow from rolling western prairies,
   The great waves gleam like emeralds capped with foam;
Then small boats hug the shore and wait for evening
   Before they venture from the lights of home.

But, when the evening comes, the lake is quiet,
   All now is silent but the loon's weird cry;
And little boats ride bravely out from shelter,
   And stars march forth across the dusky sky.

When moonlight shines at night upon the water
   And white gulls circle low on snowy wings,
We know that joys like these bring life new rapture
   And live forever in the heart that sings.

NINA PRIDE HOAG, Minneapolis

Pomme de Terre

LAC QUI PARLE

Ojibways, Chippewas, and Dakotahs, roaming
Across these virgin plains, knew well the sound
Of talking water. French-born voyageurs, combing
The wilds for trade in furs, passed here and found
The "lake which speaks" — the vocal Lac qui Parle.
Here echoes winged their way from bluff-ringed shores.
The springtimes' icebreaks, crumbling clay and marl;
The tom-toms' beating; brutal tribal wars;
The white man's marriage to these fertile prairies;
The hymns that Riggs and Williamson raised to God;
The shouts of Sibley's men — the lake's soul carries
These lusty voices born on this ageless sod.

The blue waves move in strange unmeasured bars,
And chants rise up from depths inlaid with stars.

GERTRUDE HANSON, *Island Park*

Sioux Indian Mission, Lac qui Parle

DAWN IN AN ALEXANDRIA GARDEN

Dawn crowns the day with opal diadems —
   Too lovely to be viewed without swift pain,
   That binds me like a delicate gold chain.
No flowers, poised in beauty on their stems,
Can match the hues of dawn's bright trailing hems.
   Pale lavender and pink precede a train
   Of rose and gold and saffron-tinted stain,
With all the brilliance of a thousand gems.
How happily I watch the dawn's parade
   Of gorgeous colors with new seeing eyes,
     Well knowing it has healed my bitterness.
As I behold the glowing colors fade,
   And see the sun in all its glory rise,
     I know each day holds richer promises.

LUCY-LEONE MARSCH, Alexandria

LAND OF PLENTY

(Red River Valley)

The dewy beam of morning breaks
On growing fields, like mirrored lakes;
New harmonies of nature rise
To greet the dawn of sun-kissed skies.
The tempering breath of winter's chill
Brings courage and determined will
To do our best and go our way
In honest toil from day to day.
We love these undulating plains;
We prize the yield of golden grains,
The fertile valley, scattered trees —
Divine benevolences, these!

GEORGE D. CRAIG, Angus

OUR TREES

We wait your emerald buds, that come by stealth
To blow the bugle of our northern springs.
We greet your later robes of verdant wealth
With joy — that lavish raiment summer brings.
Then, flaming hues of autumn's changing dyes
Swiftly transform this clothing at frost's call.
All these appeal, in turn, to native eyes;
Our love for home is rooted in them all.
But now, when winter's jealous winds have claimed
Your covering, you stand courageously
And fling against the evening sky, unframed,
Your rugged strength, your grace, your majesty.
Then, unadorned, your sturdy forms impart
An ecstasy that lingers in the heart.

IZELLA WILLIS DART, *Minneapolis*

WILD MOCCASINS FOR ME

Deep in a tamarack forest,
  Where people seldom go,
On carpets of moss and needles,
  The moccasin flowers grow;
Among the tamarack shadows,
  The pale green leaves unfold,
Yellowed by dainty blossoms,
  A touch of Midas-gold.
Orchids, a costly purchase,
  I never hope to see —
Wild moccasins from the swamp land
  Are far more precious to me.

CHARLOTTE BELDEN, *Rush City*

A PINE ON THE CHIPPEWA TRAIL

My head is now among the stars
But once it barely lifted
Above the moss and wintergreen
Where falling needles sifted.

The prairie schooners plodded past,
Their shrunken larders needing
Wild rabbit and fat porcupine
For little children's feeding.

Soon here and there a steeple topped
The lordly pines and birches,
And youngsters trooped to Sunday school
In homes, and rural churches.

Here wagons lumbered woodland trails;
And hunters stalked their prey
Of big game in the forest haunts,
Where moose were known to stray.

But I remain a lonely pine,
A landmark for the ages . . .
My memories are rich with lore
Engraved in history's pages.

MYRTA ALBERTSON WELLS, *Minneapolis*

FOREST PRIMEVAL PARK
(Little Falls)

Here all is still . . .
Yet the silence seems alive with sound:
The soft crumbling of earth under our feet —
Earth that holds the soul of leaves,
Dying in autumn;
And the trees giving challenge like sentinels.
O Forest Primeval, have you a secret?
We wonder, wishing some one were here
With a voice from the past to tell the story:
   Of bison grazing in the meadow,
   Of deer shyly peering through the leaves,
   And birds with sudden noise of wings
   Rising to the trees' sunny crowns.
But all is forgotten — the noise of battle,
The hunt and the kill.
Forest Primeval, your brave days are ended!
Only an echo remains, stirring our hearts.
Yet we stand in silence, awed by your splendor . . .
Then go with footsteps lighter for this quiet hour.

KATE THOMSON CURIAL, *Minneapolis*

RUNESTONE SAGA

(Kensington, 1362)

The rough-hewn stone was ready, and he knelt
To brush away the dust with calloused hand;
Not one in all the silent group but felt
The moment's import. In this empty land,
They knew, in time, their runestone would be found
And read by bearded Vikings, tall and straight
Of limb as they who stood and made no sound,
While one inscribed the story of their fate.

He measured with his eyes the rough gray stone;
And with his heart, the weary length of days
That they had come. How many moons had shone
Upon their campfires in the forest maze
Since they had known a harbor where the cries
Of welcome had been loud on every tongue,
Where men could rest beneath the bright home skies,
And all the long adventure could be sung!

No song, but stone, would speak for them; he took
The clumsy tool in awkward hands; and, when
He had engraved the year, he paused to look
Again upon those rugged uncouth men.
"8 Goths and 22 Norwegians came"—
Their saga lives upon a stone once bare.
In runic staves, he pressed their humble claim;
"Hail Mary, save from evil!" was his prayer.

Frances Lyksett, St. Paul

KENSINGTON RUNESTONE

LAKE ITASCA

ITASCA IN OCTOBER

Strange, a rock — a stone —
  could be mauve, in certain lights —
  shadows along the shore.
Chrome, the dying leaves of autumn
  on the graceful, low tree
  between the birches. . . . Peace is here —
  old, dear, and remembered.
Yellow are the birch leaves, those left,
  on long arms, reaching out like nostalgic hearts,
  hungering with loneliness.
Beneath, green still, are leaves
  sprouted from low upshoots
  in the sere, gray grass — tenacious new life —
  brought forth late last spring.
And slim and rich red, veins
  of blood, the body of the dried
  wild rosebush stands — shivering.
  Birds took all the berries.
Wine are the hazel bushes — wine
  that was left of summer — to quicken
  the clear, thin air of autumn, shot through
  with cold October sunshine.
Beyond, the quiet blue lake stretches wider
  than tired eyes can see —
  mauve the shadows of a far shore — swept —
  and still, as is the heart.

NELLIE MANLEY BUCK, *Coleraine*

LAKE ITASCA

In a deep and virgin forest,
Where the hidden wild things grow,
Is a lake of charm and beauty,
Holding stars and sunset glow.

This is lovely Lake Itasca,
Like a bowl of jewelled jade,
With its curving broken shoreline,
Where the cranes and plovers wade.

Here the thirsty deer and beaver
And the timid speckled fawn
Come in trembling fear and wonder,
In the rosy light of dawn.

All is ancient as the ice age,
Reaching back from year to year,
Drowsing here until discovered —
Lake Itasca, deep and clear!

GERTIE M. ORCUTT, *Minneapolis*

Douglas Lodge

Itasca State Park

SPRING OF THE MISSISSIPPI

When Polaris twirled this globe,
He tossed a star to Minnesota;
Its rays shone forth on all the earth.
In the deep of Lake Itasca,
A regal spring lay dormant
Until the north star lit the depths
And roused it from its slumber.
Trembling with the ecstasy of life,
Rejoicing in its freedom,
In an avalanche of power,
It rode in torrents
Over the Falls of St. Anthony.
Widening its circles
And gaining in momentum,
It conquered whirling pools
And raging rapids
In cyclonic cruel Pepin.
With river moods,
Alluring kindred waters,
It rushes ever onward
In its longing to be one
With the friendly southern sea.

KOKAB H. A. MacCUTCHEON,
Minneapolis

GULL LAKE

If, now and then, man ceased his endless climb
To self-appointed goals, and left the town. . . .
If he forsook the cruel trampling ways
Of stony-hearted pavements, went to walk
Beside the waters of this quiet lake,
His feet would feel the firmness of the shore
That slopes into a green eternity;
And he would see the pebbles glistening
Among the wave-dipped ridges of the sand.
And farther up the beach, the blue-green clay
Might there replace the gold beneath a cliff;
A frog might leap from out the sodden leaves
To lose itself among the lake shore reeds.

Then for just a while, man would know freedom
From all his furious rivalries and fears;
The soothing coolness of the air would ease
The weariness, the fever . . .he would see
How puny are his strivings, and how futile,
When calm unmindful nature goes her way.

MARJORIE MILLS, *Minneapolis*

ORIGIN OF LEECH LAKE

(Chippewa Legend)

Long — oh, long ago, Wyona,
  Fairest maid of Indian lore,
And her mother, called Demoya,
  Lived where no one lived before.
But, alas, an evil spirit
  Stole Wyona, when alone,
And he took her to his wigwam
  That was made as strong as stone.

Then a spirit emissary,
  Who from Hiawatha came,
Gave her a pebble, hard as flint is.
  He, the one of magic fame,
Bade her make a spearhead of it
  And to strike the earth. Out gushed
Waters full of seething eddies
  Till a deep wide lake had rushed.

Then the maid, who fled her captor
  And the water flooding round,
Climbed the stony bank above it
  Till she stood upon the ground.
Daily now the buried spirit
  Like a lion from his lair,
As the wind goes raging madly,
  Voices anger on the air.

TAYLOR ALEXANDER, *St. Paul*

RESERVATION SCHOOL
(Red Lake)

Each greying day I pause awhile
Upon the threshhold of my room
And school my lips to hold a smile -
A daily face I must assume.

Red Lake lies dormant under ice,
Uncompromising as the truth . . .
My thoughts go scuttling round like mice —
What should one now expect of youth?

"Not what you . . . but what they learn . . ."
So through the door, thought-mice with me . . .
I have a mind to be most stern,
And heart to loose them — set youth free.

MABEL ERICKSEN ANDERSEN, *Red Lake*

AT LAKE SULLIVAN

I like
The giant pine,
That leans against the sky,
Fearless and tall, braving the winds
And storms.

May I,
Like this great tree,
Stand firm, with head unbowed,
And calmly meet the buffetings
Of life!

JOSEPHA CONTOSKI, *Minneapolis*

SONG OF THE CROW WING

Sing, little river; the first spring leaves
Yellow the gaunt brown branches;
Jade is the carpet that April weaves
Over the woods and ranches.
Sing a gay song of the oriole,
Building a nest in a leafy bowl.

Push, little river, the wild rose buds;
Yellow the roads with clover;
Churn your dark ripples to foamy suds —
June is a gypsy rover!
Cornfields are tasseling, row on row;
Bobolinks swing where the cat-tails grow.

Glint, little river; the maples flame —
Crimson, the leaves, and copper;
Goldenrod burned as the sumac came . . .
Who but the frost could stop her?
Blackbirds are twittering . . . crows reply . . .
Geese are a wedge in a hazy sky.

Dream, little river; the snow lies thick,
Drifting the roads and hollows;
Time for the lanthorn and candlewick —
Short is the day that follows!
Sing of the roots and the bulbs that wait
Rain's tap tapping at April's gate.

MARGARETTE BALL DICKSON, *Staples*

SEEN NEAR BRAINERD

Sun-inflamed,
The maple
Erupts, in violent light,
A wild volcanic madness
So bright
That sober spruce around
Catch it
And sway in slow
Deliberate delight
Of natures, stern
And more profound.

JOHAN S. EGILSRUD, *University of Minnesota*

MINNESOTA AUTUMN

We saw the street lamp's mellow light
Reveal a yellow tree at night,
More beautiful than sun at noon
Shining on forests late in June.
The lamp, the tree, the late romance
Precipitate their molten gold
Like falling leaves and smiles that dance
On features growing wise . . . and old.

KATHERINE M. MILLER, *Rochester*

PAUL BUNYAN

Paul Bunyan's ax makes the woodlands ring,
And we hear his blue ox bellowing;
As the winds sweep over lakes and pines,
Paul lives again in folk-lore lines.

DE ETTE CENFIELD GENUNG, *Minneapolis*

AT BURNTSIDE LAKE

Breathless, on this hard fist of land clenched far into open waters,
I look long into wind and wave . . . and sense
An overwhelming denseness in these depths —
As of a herd of elephants lumbering toward me:
Silver-fissured masses are bulging, heaving, pushing, flank against flank,
Topped by lesser swells that come bobbing, nodding — their rhythms
    broken by ivory flashes in wanton toss. . . .
While in ominous undercurrent sounds a muffled pounding, pounding,
    pounding. . . .

I choke! I chill! I shiver, shrink in fright
At nature thus unleashed, this terrible in wild stampede. . . .
Lumbering, heaving, pushing, pounding from afar; then nearer, ever
    nearer — oh, too near!
    — nudging at my self-esteem,
    — chortling at the smug decorum of my city ways,
    — threatening to loose my land-grip here on this windy point!
Oh! There is too much of thickness here for sight, for sound, for breath!
And I must go — must go at once, to the cabin's comfort and human com-
    pany!

SELMA SAARI EVANS, *Minneota*

Scenic State Park

RED RIVER OX CARTS

Squink, squank, the big wheels went around—
Squank, squunk, a creaking, croaking sound—

A prairie song of wood and rawhide leather,
A commerce song against mud-sloughs and weather.
Slow, plodding oxen pulled the great wheels on—
A thousand pounds of furs between two wheels,
A thousand wheels' protesting wooden squeals,
And, deeply, wide rims bogged through history.

Half Chippewa and picturesque of form,
The drivers knew the blizzard way of storm,
Knew prairie grass and smell of weather wind,
Knew first warm breath of spring for measuring,
Knew all the lusty ways of treasuring
The rugged days and stinging nights of cold.

Now voyageurs with scarlet sash are gone,
New trade routes web the smoke-stained rose of dawn,
And cities clang with progress then begun.
But ever faint within the hoarse wind's cry
Rides the sound of ox carts burdening by;
And, muddy-red, the sash of river bends.

Squink, squank, the noise reeled miles around—
Squank, squunk, a loud, laborious sound.

MERLE FULLMER, *South St. Paul*

*Buffalo River
State Park*

LAKE OF THE WOODS

I walk along the empty shore,
Where quiet pools are ringed with foam
  And tall reeds form an outer guard.
  No other human step has marred
    The rippled pattern of the sand,
    Or rent the silence of this land.

I cannot see across the lake,
For, mile on mile, the waters spread;
  And in this solitude I find
  Only the creatures of my mind,
    Or gulls who fly in spiral rings
    Upon their soundless snowy wings.

This morning I can almost think
This is the first day of creation,
  And only birds and beasts and I
  Have ever known this lake and sky;
    And any moment I may see
    Adam and Eve beneath a tree.

NATALIE FITZ-PATRICK SAGAR, *Minneapolis*

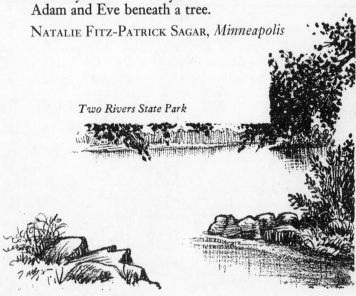

Two Rivers State Park

RED RIVER VALLEY

Once on your bosom the cold blue waters
Of Lake Agassiz rolled;
And, as the eons passed,
You sucked into your hungry pores
The rich deposits that it held
And buried them deep within your heart.

The sun, companion of your greediness,
Sent beams to coax the water from its bed
And left the garnered wealth to you.
And there you lay for ages more.
The lash of chilling wind and stubborn snow
Worked with the alchemist to give
The richer earth its virgin loveliness.

Your only rival is the valley of the Nile,
Where Cleopatra lured Mark Antony,
Although your fame requires no queen
Or warrior to make it live.

Your tempting stores were like a magnet
To pioneers who scarred your form
With the first gash of the plow
And gave you seeds to nurture.
Now you hold within your breast
Their sacred dust, impregnating still
The prairie which they long had loved.

MARY MacFarlane Wooley, *St. Paul*

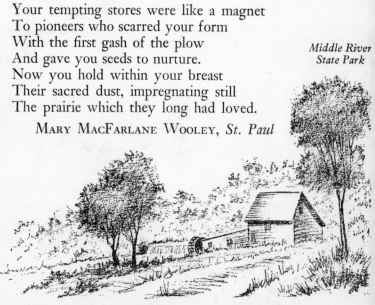

*Middle River
State Park*

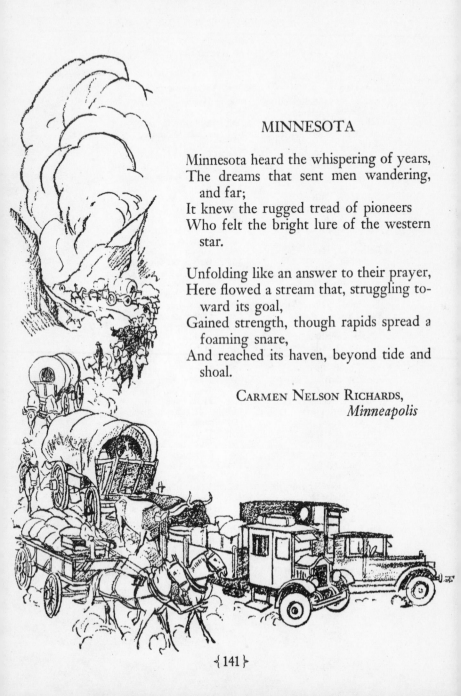

MINNESOTA

Minnesota heard the whispering of years,
The dreams that sent men wandering,
  and far;
It knew the rugged tread of pioneers
Who felt the bright lure of the western
  star.

Unfolding like an answer to their prayer,
Here flowed a stream that, struggling toward its goal,
Gained strength, though rapids spread a
  foaming snare,
And reached its haven, beyond tide and
  shoal.

CARMEN NELSON RICHARDS,
Minneapolis

INDEX

INSERT ILLUSTRATIONS

IN APPRECIATION

The editor and publisher wishes to thank those whose generous cooperation has given valuable assistance during the progress of the work on this volume:

Jessie Goddard Broman, Dr. Edward Collins Downing, Lillian G. Atcherson, Victoria Janda, Frances Greenleaf Jensen, Emma Kinney Whaley, Katherine McCormack, Marjorie W. Brachlow, Nan Fitz-Patrick, Gertrude Hanson, and all others who graciously contributed to this book.

We are also deeply grateful to the following who have given us permission to use their cuts:

The Division of State Parks of the Department of Conservation for the authentic cuts of State Parks

The Bureau of Conservation Information

The State Department of Business Development

The Minnesota State Automobile Association

The Great Northern Railway Company

The Civic and Commerce Associations of Minneapolis, St. Paul, and Rochester

General Mills, Inc.

The University of Minnesota News Service

The Friend Magazine

Minneapolis Public Library
and many of the commercial printers of Minneapolis and St. Paul.

* * *

May this book be a symbol of gratitude for those who, through sacrifice and courage, have made it possible to live in Minnesota in peace and harmony.

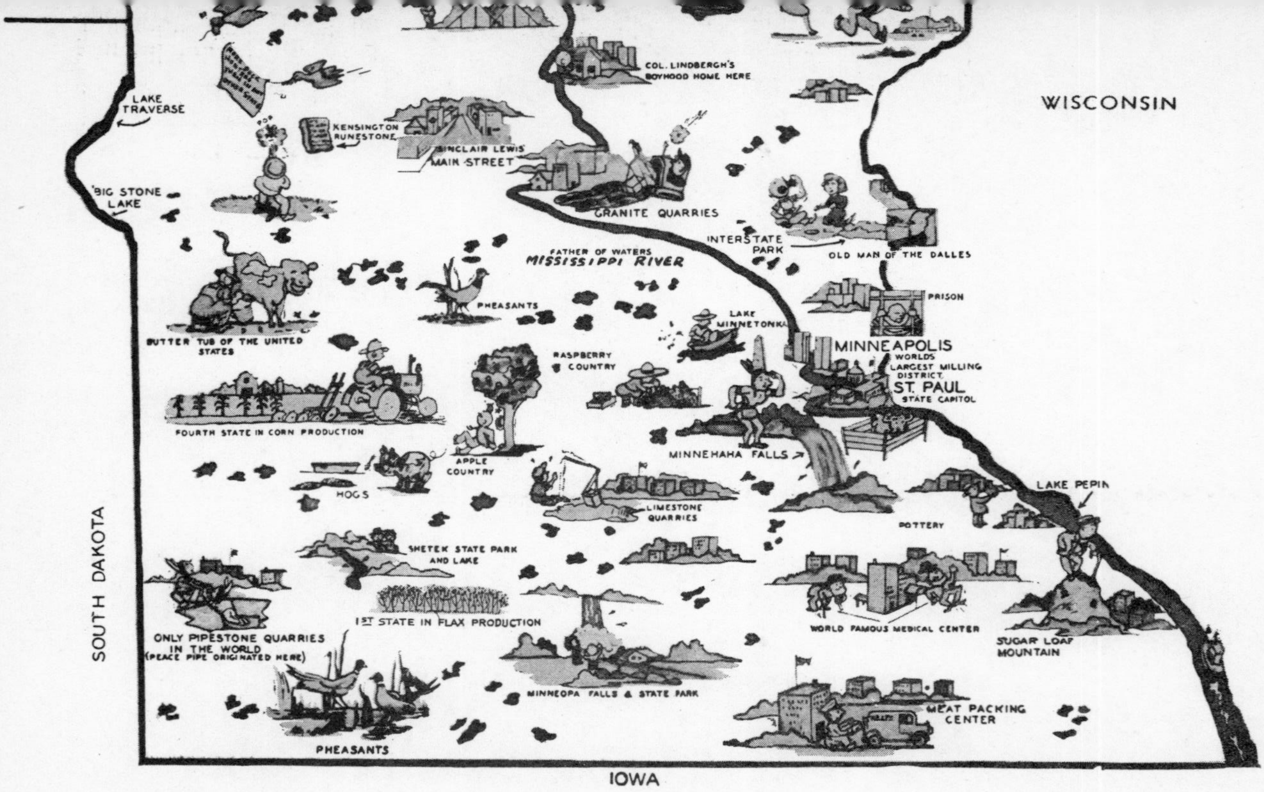

WISCONSIN
LAKE TRAVERSE
BIG STONE LAKE
KENSINGTON RUNESTONE
SINCLAIR LEWIS' MAIN STREET
COL. LINDBERGH'S BOYHOOD HOME HERE
GRANITE QUARRIES
INTERSTATE PARK
OLD MAN OF THE DALLES
FATHER OF WATERS
MISSISSIPPI RIVER
PHEASANTS
BUTTER TUB OF THE UNITED STATES
PRISON
LAKE MINNETONKA
MINNEAPOLIS
WORLDS LARGEST MILLING DISTRICT
ST. PAUL
STATE CAPITOL
RASPBERRY COUNTRY
FOURTH STATE IN CORN PRODUCTION
APPLE COUNTRY
MINNEHAHA FALLS
HOGS
LIMESTONE QUARRIES
LAKE PEPIN
POTTERY
SHETEK STATE PARK AND LAKE
SOUTH DAKOTA
1ST STATE IN FLAX PRODUCTION
WORLD FAMOUS MEDICAL CENTER
ONLY PIPESTONE QUARRIES IN THE WORLD
(PEACE PIPE ORIGINATED HERE)
SUGAR LOAF MOUNTAIN
MINNEOPA FALLS & STATE PARK
MEAT PACKING CENTER
PHEASANTS
IOWA